# How to Make Money Online with ChatGPT: The Ultimate Guide for Entrepreneurs and Freelancers

ChatGPT Millionaire book blueprint: Side Hustles and Business Ideas for 2025

**ALEX HARPER**

# Contents

| | |
|---|---|
| Foreword | vii |
| 1. INTRODUCTION TO CHATGPT AND GENERATIVE AI. | 1 |
| 1.1 Overview of ChatGPT and Its Journey to GPT-5 | 2 |
| 1.2 Understanding Generative AI and Its Influence Across Industries | 3 |
| 1.3 The Rising Role of AI in Reshaping the Economy | 4 |
| 2. GETTING STARTED WITH CHATGPT | 7 |
| 2.1 Setting Up ChatGPT for Personal and Professional Use | 7 |
| 2.2 Navigating the User Interface and Essential Features | 9 |
| 2.3 The Art of Prompt Engineering | 10 |
| 2.4 Advanced Usage Tips | 11 |
| 2.5 Troubleshooting and Overcoming Challenges | 13 |
| 2.6 Practical Exercises | 13 |
| 3. EXPLORING CHATGPT'S FULL POTENTIAL | 15 |
| 3.1 Creating High-Quality Content | 15 |
| 3.2 Enhancing Productivity in Coding | 17 |
| 3.3 Building Unique Applications | 18 |
| 3.4 Generating Creative Works | 19 |
| 3.5 Industry-Specific Applications | 20 |
| 3.6 Enhancing Collaboration with Teams | 21 |
| 3.7 Prompt Templates and Libraries | 22 |
| Troubleshooting Common Challenges | 27 |
| General Tips for Troubleshooting | 31 |
| 4. COMPREHENSIVE STRATEGIES FOR INCOME GENERATION | 33 |
| 4.1 Offering Freelance Writing and Content Services | 33 |
| 4.2 AI-Driven Digital Marketing: Unlocking Opportunities | 35 |

| | |
|---|---|
| 4.3 Creating and Selling Digital Products | 36 |
| 4.4.1 Building an Affiliate Marketing Blog | 37 |
| 4.5 Scaling E-Commerce with ChatGPT | 38 |
| 4.6 Combining ChatGPT with Automation and APIs | 38 |
| 4.7 Advanced Monetization Strategies | 39 |
| 4.8 Ethical Considerations for Monetization | 39 |
| **5. ADVANCED AI INTEGRATION FOR PROFIT** | **41** |
| 5.1 Automating Workflows for Efficiency and Scalability | 41 |
| 5.2 Combining ChatGPT with APIs | 43 |
| 5.4 Using AI Insights for Business Analytics | 46 |
| 5.5 Innovative AI-Driven Business Models | 46 |
| 5.7 Real-World Success Stories | 47 |
| **6. UNLOCKING THE HIDDEN POWER OF PROMPTS** | **49** |
| Prompts for Every Niche | 49 |
| 6.1 Content Creation | 49 |
| 6.2 Coding | 50 |
| 6.3 Marketing | 52 |
| 6.4 Personal Productivity | 53 |
| 6.5 Business Growth | 54 |
| Unique and Unexpected Ideas for Using ChatGPT | 55 |
| 6.7 Designing Board Games and Escape Room Narratives | 57 |
| 6.8 Creating Personalized Greeting Card Messages for Sale | 58 |
| 6.9 Generating Engaging Online Quizzes and Trivia | 59 |
| 6.10 Offering Niche AI Services Like Grant Writing or Legal Drafts | 60 |
| Tips You've Never Thought Of: Leveraging ChatGPT for Unique Opportunities | 62 |
| 6.11 Using AI to Identify Untapped Markets or Trending Business Ideas | 62 |
| 6.12 Generating Press Releases and Media Kits for Startups | 63 |
| 6.13 Creating Custom ChatGPT Personas for Specific Industries | 64 |

| 7. CASE STUDIES AND SUCCESS STORIES | 67 |
|---|---|
| 8. ETHICAL CONSIDERATIONS AND AI CHALLENGES | 74 |
| 8.1 Navigating Ethical Dilemmas in AI-Generated Work | 74 |
| 8.2 Addressing Plagiarism, Intellectual Property, and Authenticity | 76 |
| 8.3 Managing Client and Audience Expectations | 77 |
| 8.4 Preparing for Ethical Challenges in Emerging AI Applications | 78 |
| 8.5 Actionable Tips for Responsible AI Use | 79 |
| 8.6 Real-World Examples of Ethical Challenges and Solutions | 80 |
| 9. FUTURE TRENDS AND OPPORTUNITIES IN AI | 81 |
| 9.1 The Evolving Landscape of Generative AI Tools | 81 |
| 9.2 Emerging Applications in Key Industries | 83 |
| 9.3 Preparing for a World Integrated with AI | 85 |
| 10. RESOURCES AND TOOLS FOR AMPLIFYING CHATGPT'S FUNCTIONALITY | 88 |
| 10.1 Must-Have AI Tools to Amplify ChatGPT's Functionality | 88 |
| 10.2 Recommended Platforms for Freelancing and Selling Content | 90 |
| 10.3 Communities, Blogs, and Forums for Continued Learning | 91 |
| 11. CONCLUSION AND NEXT STEPS FOR AI-POWERED SUCCESS | 95 |
| 11.1 Recap of Key Takeaways | 95 |
| 11.2 Actionable Next Steps | 96 |
| 11.3 Inspiration to Innovate and Adapt | 98 |
| 11.4 Your Roadmap to AI-Powered Success | 99 |
| Frequently Asked Questions | 101 |

# Foreword

The world is changing faster than ever before. Every day, we hear about breakthroughs in technology reshaping industries, disrupting norms, and creating opportunities that once seemed impossible. At the forefront of this revolution is artificial intelligence—and among the most transformative tools is ChatGPT.

When I first encountered ChatGPT, I was intrigued by its ability to craft words with precision, generate ideas with creativity, and solve problems with efficiency. But the more I used it, the more I realized something extraordinary: ChatGPT isn't just a tool—it's a gateway to possibility. It's a collaborator, a productivity booster, and for those who know how to wield its power, a life-changing income generator.

This book, *How to Make Money Online with ChatGPT: The Ultimate Guide for Entrepreneurs and Freelancers,* is your guide to navigating this exciting new frontier. Whether you're a budding entrepreneur, an ambitious freelancer, or someone looking to unlock financial freedom, this book lays out a clear, actionable path to harnessing the potential of AI. Alex Harper doesn't just explain how to use ChatGPT—he shows you how to transform it into your most valuable business partner.

# Foreword

In these pages, you'll discover how ChatGPT can help you generate passive income, kickstart profitable side hustles, and scale your efforts faster than ever before. From crafting the best prompts to uncovering the most lucrative business ideas for 2025, every chapter is packed with insights, strategies, and inspiration to empower you to take charge of your financial destiny.

But this isn't just a book about making money. It's about adapting to the future, embracing innovation, and thinking creatively in a world where AI is becoming a driving force in our lives. By the time you turn the final page, you'll be equipped not only with practical knowledge but with the confidence to seize opportunities in this ever-evolving digital landscape.

The future belongs to those who see possibilities where others see uncertainty. By picking up this book, you've already taken the first step toward creating the life you've always dreamed of. So, let's dive in, explore what's possible, and build something incredible together.

The future is yours to shape—let ChatGPT help you write it.

# Chapter 1
# Introduction to ChatGPT and Generative AI.

The world of artificial intelligence (AI) has witnessed remarkable progress in recent years, and at the forefront of this revolution is **ChatGPT**, OpenAI's conversational AI model. Designed to understand and generate human-like text, ChatGPT has opened doors to a multitude of possibilities across industries, transforming how we communicate, work, and innovate. In this chapter, we'll explore the evolution of ChatGPT, delve into the broader implications of generative AI, and examine how AI is reshaping the global economy.

## 1.1 Overview of ChatGPT and Its Journey to GPT-5

ChatGPT, developed by OpenAI, is part of the GPT (Generative Pre-trained Transformer) family, a series of increasingly sophisticated language models. Let's take a closer look at its evolutionary journey:

- **GPT-1 to GPT-3:** These earlier iterations introduced the core concept of generative AI: the ability to predict and generate coherent, contextually relevant text based on input. GPT-3, in particular, demonstrated an uncanny ability to perform a wide variety of tasks—from writing essays to coding snippets—earning widespread recognition.
- **ChatGPT:** Built on the foundation of GPT-3.5 and beyond, ChatGPT refined the conversational aspect of AI, focusing on understanding user intent, maintaining context over multiple exchanges, and generating human-like responses. ChatGPT bridged the gap between a static tool and a dynamic conversational assistant.
- **GPT-4 and GPT-5:** Each subsequent version improved significantly in terms of contextual understanding, language fluency, and creative capabilities. By GPT-5, the model became even more adept at tackling complex queries, integrating real-time feedback, and performing nuanced tasks such as emotional tone detection and adaptive learning.

**Example Use Cases of ChatGPT Today**

- **Personal Assistants:** Scheduling, reminders, and email drafting.
- **Content Creation:** Articles, blog posts, marketing copy, and scripts.
- **Coding:** Debugging, algorithm creation, and optimization.
- **Customer Service:** Automated yet personalized responses for businesses.

## 1.2 Understanding Generative AI and Its Influence Across Industries

At its core, generative AI, exemplified by ChatGPT, uses vast datasets and advanced machine learning techniques to produce human-like outputs. Unlike traditional AI, which focuses on rule-based systems or pattern recognition, generative AI creates new content, opening up revolutionary possibilities.

**Generative AI in Action**

- **Content Creation:** AI-generated articles, graphics, and videos are redefining the media landscape, making production faster and more cost-effective.
- **Healthcare:** AI systems assist in medical research, patient diagnosis, and drug discovery, accelerating advancements in treatment.
- **Education:** Personalized AI tutors adapt to students' learning styles, providing tailored lessons and practice exercises.
- **Finance:** AI optimizes stock trading algorithms, analyzes risks, and generates reports in seconds.
- **Entertainment:** From crafting compelling storylines to generating music, AI is driving innovation in creative industries.

**The Competitive Edge of Generative AI**

Generative AI is not just a tool—it's a transformative force that gives businesses and individuals an edge by enhancing creativity, productivity, and problem-solving. For example:

- **Startups** leverage AI to quickly create marketing campaigns, cutting costs while increasing reach.
- **Freelancers** use AI to handle repetitive tasks like drafting proposals, leaving more time for strategic work.
- **Corporate Teams** rely on AI for brainstorming ideas, analyzing large datasets, and automating workflows.

## 1.3 The Rising Role of AI in Reshaping the Economy

AI is reshaping how businesses operate, creating new economic opportunities while disrupting traditional markets. Here's a closer look at its impact:

### 1.3.1 Job Transformation

While fears of job displacement often dominate discussions, AI is also creating entirely new roles. Skills in **AI development, prompt engineering, and AI integration** are in high demand, and industries are adapting to these shifts by training workers for hybrid roles where humans and AI collaborate.

- **Example:** A content marketer might use ChatGPT to draft blog posts, allowing them to focus more on strategy and audience engagement.

### 1.3.2 Democratization of Resources

AI levels the playing field by providing affordable tools that were once accessible only to large enterprises. Freelancers, small business owners, and creators can now compete in global markets using AI for:

- Professional-grade designs.
- High-quality content production.
- Market analysis and forecasting.

. . .

### 1.3.3 AI-Powered Startups and Entrepreneurship

Generative AI lowers the barrier to entry for starting a business. Entrepreneurs can:
- Generate ideas and conduct feasibility studies in minutes.
- Automate customer interactions with AI chatbots.
- Scale operations without significant overhead costs.

**Case in Point:** A solo entrepreneur can launch a successful online store using AI for product descriptions, inventory management, and customer support, all while maintaining a lean team.

### Actionable Guidance: Embracing AI as a Game-Changer

Understanding the potential of ChatGPT and generative AI is only the first step. Here are three actionable ways to start integrating AI into your workflow:

- **Experiment with ChatGPT**: Begin with simple prompts to explore its capabilities. For instance, try generating a blog outline or brainstorming ideas for a side hustle.
- **Identify Use Cases in Your Field**: Reflect on repetitive tasks in your work or business that could be automated or enhanced using ChatGPT. Examples include drafting emails, creating reports, or generating social media posts.
- **Stay Informed**: AI evolves rapidly. Regularly explore updates to ChatGPT and other generative AI tools to stay ahead of the curve.

### Conclusion

ChatGPT and generative AI are not just technological marvels—they are tools that empower individuals and businesses to innovate, optimize, and thrive in an increasingly AI-driven world. Whether you're a freelancer, entrepreneur, or corporate professional, understanding and leveraging AI can unlock unparalleled opportunities.

In the next chapter, we'll dive into **how to get started with ChatGPT**, ensuring you're equipped to harness its potential for personal and professional growth. From setting up the tool to mastering its features, you'll gain the foundational knowledge needed to unlock its full potential.

*Get ready to take the first steps toward your journey as a ChatGPT-powered innovator!*

# Chapter 2
# Getting Started with ChatGPT

Getting started with ChatGPT is an exciting journey that can transform how you approach personal projects and professional tasks. This chapter is your comprehensive guide to understanding how to set up, navigate, and utilize ChatGPT effectively. By mastering these foundational elements, you'll be ready to harness its capabilities for everything from productivity to innovation.

## 2.1 Setting Up ChatGPT for Personal and Professional Use

Before diving into its features, it's essential to set up ChatGPT properly to suit your specific goals. This process ensures that you're equipped to use the tool efficiently and effectively.

### 2.1.1 Choosing the Right Plan
ChatGPT offers different plans tailored to diverse needs:
- **Free Plan**: Ideal for casual users exploring the tool's capabili-

ties. It allows basic access but may have limited availability during peak times and slower processing speeds.

- **Pro Plan**: Designed for professionals, offering faster response times, priority access during high-traffic periods, and access to advanced versions like GPT-4 or GPT-5.
- **API Access**: Essential for developers or businesses aiming to integrate ChatGPT into custom applications or workflows.

**Example Scenario**:

- A student might start with the free tier to generate study notes or research summaries.
- A content creator would benefit from the Pro Plan for faster access and enhanced output quality.
- A startup could use API access to deploy ChatGPT as a customer service chatbot on their website.

### 2.1.2 Device Compatibility and Integration

ChatGPT is available across platforms, ensuring flexibility for users:

- **Web Interface**: Accessible on desktops and laptops for long-form content creation and detailed queries.
- **Mobile App**: Convenient for quick responses or tasks on the go.
- **Integration with Tools**: Use ChatGPT alongside platforms like Microsoft Teams, Slack, or Google Docs to enhance collaboration.

**Pro Tip**: If you're planning to use ChatGPT regularly, consider bookmarking the platform on your browser or installing the app for easy access.

### 2.1.3 Customizing Settings for Efficiency

Adjusting ChatGPT settings can significantly improve your experience:

- **Conversation History**: Enable or disable this feature based on your privacy preferences.
- **Output Style**: Experiment with settings to adjust the tone and format of responses.
- **Notifications**: Configure alerts for updates, especially if you're using ChatGPT in a collaborative or professional setting.

**Example Use Case**:

A freelance writer may enable conversation history to revisit previous drafts or refine ongoing projects.

## 2.2 Navigating the User Interface and Essential Features

Once you're set up, the next step is understanding the user interface and features that make ChatGPT an intuitive and powerful tool.

### 2.2.1 Key Components of the Interface

The ChatGPT interface is designed to be user-friendly:

1 **Input Field**: This is where you type prompts or questions. Think of it as a conversation starter or command center.

2 **Response Panel**: Displays ChatGPT's replies. You can interact further by refining the output or asking follow-up questions.

3 **Sidebar/History Panel**: Allows you to revisit past conversations (if enabled).

4 **Settings/Account Menu**: Access billing, adjust privacy settings, or explore additional features.

**Real-World Example**:

- A marketer could use the input field to request social media captions and then refine those captions based on the audience or platform.

### 2.2.2 Core Features to Leverage

Here's a breakdown of essential ChatGPT features that will enhance your experience:

- **Contextual Memory**: ChatGPT remembers the context of your conversation during a session, enabling coherent and progressive discussions.
  - *Example*: If you're brainstorming for a marketing campaign, you can ask for tagline ideas, then follow up with, "Expand on tagline #3."
- **Tone Adjustment**: Modify the tone of the response to match your target audience.
  - *Example*: "Rewrite this explanation in a casual, conversational tone suitable for teenagers."
- **Output Customization**: Specify output requirements like word count, format, or level of detail.
  - *Example*: "Summarize this article in 150 words" or "Generate a 5-slide PowerPoint outline."

## 2.3 The Art of Prompt Engineering

Prompt engineering is the cornerstone of effective ChatGPT usage. The quality of your results depends on the clarity, detail, and structure of your prompts.

### 2.3.1 Anatomy of a Strong Prompt

A good prompt includes:

1 **Context**: Explain the purpose or scenario for your query.
2 **Specific Instructions**: Clearly state what you need.
3 **Constraints or Style Preferences**: Define tone, format, length, or audience.

**Weak Prompt**: "Write about AI." **Strong Prompt**: "Write a 300-word article about how AI is transforming small businesses, focusing on cost reduction and customer service improvement. Use an informative tone."

### 2.3.2 Iterative Prompt Refinement

The first response might not always be perfect. Here's how to refine:

- **Follow-Up Questions**: Ask ChatGPT to clarify or elaborate.
  - *Example*: "Can you provide examples of cost reduction strategies in retail using AI?"
- **Feedback for Revisions**: Specify adjustments.
  - *Example*: "Make this more concise" or "Rewrite with a focus on small e-commerce stores."

### 2.3.3 Advanced Prompting Techniques

1. **Role-Specific Prompts**: Instruct ChatGPT to act as a particular persona.
   - *Example*: "You are a career coach. Give advice to someone switching from teaching to tech."
2. **Layered Prompts**: Break complex tasks into sequential steps.
   - *Example*: "First, create an outline for a blog on AI in healthcare. Then write the introduction."
3. **Comparative Prompts**: Request side-by-side options for better decision-making.
   - *Example*: "Provide two versions of a product description: one for a professional audience and one for a casual audience."

## 2.4 Advanced Usage Tips

Once you've mastered the basics, explore these strategies to elevate your ChatGPT experience:

### 2.4.1 Collaborative Applications
• Share outputs with team members for feedback or collaboration.

  ○ *Example*: Use ChatGPT to draft a project proposal, then refine it with colleagues.

### 2.4.2 Integrating with Productivity Tools
• Combine ChatGPT with tools like **Notion**, **Trello**, or **Slack** for seamless integration into project workflows.

  ○ *Example*: Use Zapier to automate task creation in Trello based on ChatGPT-generated content.

### 2.4.3 Experimenting with Diverse Use Cases
The versatility of ChatGPT allows it to adapt to various scenarios:

**1 Personal Productivity**:

  ○ Plan meals: "Create a week-long meal plan for a vegetarian on a budget."

  ○ Organize travel: "Draft a 5-day itinerary for Rome, including cultural activities."

**2 Education**:

  ○ Summarize articles: "Summarize this research paper in layman's terms."

  ○ Generate quizzes: "Create a 10-question quiz about World War II."

**3 Creative Projects**:

  ○ Write poetry: "Compose a sonnet about the beauty of nature."

  ○ Design stories: "Outline a children's story about a curious robot."

## 2.5 Troubleshooting and Overcoming Challenges

ChatGPT is powerful, but like any tool, it has limitations. Here's how to address common challenges:

### 2.5.1 Dealing with Ambiguity

If responses are vague or unclear, provide more specific details in your follow-up prompt.
- *Example*: Instead of "What are some good business ideas?" try, "Suggest 5 low-cost business ideas for someone with graphic design skills."

### 2.5.2 Verifying Outputs

ChatGPT can occasionally provide inaccurate information. Cross-check facts, especially for technical or factual outputs.

### 2.5.3 Managing Complex Tasks

Break down larger tasks into smaller prompts for better clarity and results.
- *Example*: Instead of "Write a 50-page eBook on AI," start with, "Create a table of contents for an eBook on AI applications in education."

## 2.6 Practical Exercises

Here are hands-on exercises to practice and refine your ChatGPT skills:

**1 Simple Task**:
Prompt: "Write a professional email requesting a meeting with a client about project updates."

**2 Intermediate Task**:

Prompt: "Create a content calendar with 10 ideas for a tech blog targeting startups."

**3 Advanced Task**:

Prompt: "Write a script for a 3-minute YouTube video explaining how AI can improve productivity for freelancers."

**Conclusion**

Starting with ChatGPT is more than just learning how to use the tool—it's about understanding how to tailor it to your unique goals and workflows. From setting up your account to mastering prompt engineering, this chapter has provided you with the skills and insights needed to take full advantage of ChatGPT's capabilities.

In the next chapter, we'll explore **how to unlock ChatGPT's full potential**, diving deeper into its ability to create content, code, and more. Prepare to transform your workflows and see what's truly possible with this powerful AI assistant!

# Chapter 3
# Exploring ChatGPT's Full Potential

ChatGPT is more than a conversational tool—it's a versatile AI powerhouse capable of revolutionizing workflows, generating creative outputs, and optimizing complex processes. In this chapter, we'll explore how ChatGPT can be used across a variety of domains, from creating content and enhancing productivity to building innovative applications. With actionable insights and detailed examples, you'll learn how to harness the full potential of ChatGPT to elevate your projects and goals.

## 3.1 Creating High-Quality Content

One of ChatGPT's most valuable applications is content creation. Whether you're writing blogs, articles, or video scripts, ChatGPT can assist at every stage, from brainstorming to final edits.

### 3.1.1 Generating Blog Posts and Articles

ChatGPT excels at drafting blogs and articles tailored to specific topics, audiences, and styles. To achieve high-quality outputs:

**1 Provide Clear Instructions**: Start with a prompt that includes the topic, tone, and word count.

- *Example Prompt*: "Write a 1,000-word blog post about the benefits of remote work, targeting HR professionals. Use a formal tone."

**2 Use Iterative Refinement**: If the output is too generic, follow up with:

- "Focus more on statistics and real-world examples."
- "Expand on the challenges of employee engagement in remote settings."

**3 Optimize for SEO**: Request keyword-rich headings and meta descriptions.

- *Prompt*: "Add SEO-friendly subheadings and a meta description for this article."

### 3.1.2 Crafting Video Scripts

Video content is more engaging than ever, and ChatGPT can streamline scriptwriting:

**1 Generate a Script Outline**:

- *Prompt*: "Create a 5-minute video script outline for a YouTube video on 'Top 5 AI Tools for Freelancers.'"
- Output:

1 Introduction: Briefly introduce AI's relevance to freelancers.
2 Overview of Tool #1 (e.g., ChatGPT).
3 Features and benefits of Tool #2 (e.g., Canva).
4 Conclude with a call-to-action.

**2 Expand Each Section**:

- *Follow-Up Prompt*: "Write a detailed script for the introduction."

### 3.1.3 Developing Social Media Content

ChatGPT can craft compelling social media posts:

- **Short Posts**:
  - *Prompt*: "Write a 280-character tweet about why businesses should adopt AI."
- **Content Series**:
  - *Prompt*: "Create a week-long LinkedIn campaign about AI-driven productivity hacks."

**Pro Tip**: Request multiple variations of posts to A/B test effectiveness.

## 3.2 Enhancing Productivity in Coding

ChatGPT is a game-changer for developers. From generating code snippets to debugging and optimization, it simplifies complex programming tasks.

### 3.2.1 Writing Code

ChatGPT supports various programming languages and can write functional code based on your specifications:

**1 Basic Functionality**:
  - *Prompt*: "Write a Python function that calculates the factorial of a number."
  - Output:

```python
def factorial(n):
    if n == 0:
        return 1
    else:
        return n * factorial(n-1)
```

**2 Advanced Applications**:
  - *Prompt*: "Build a basic HTML form for user registration, including fields for name, email, and password."

### 3.2.2 Debugging Code

Debugging is a time-consuming process that ChatGPT can accelerate:

• *Prompt*: "Debug this Python code for calculating prime numbers. It's throwing an error when input is 1."

• Follow-Up: "Explain why the error occurred and provide a corrected version."

### 3.2.3 Optimizing Algorithms

ChatGPT can suggest performance improvements:

• *Prompt*: "Optimize this sorting algorithm to reduce time complexity."

• *Output*: ChatGPT might recommend switching from bubble sort to quicksort or implementing a more efficient data structure.

## 3.3 Building Unique Applications

Beyond individual tasks, ChatGPT can assist in creating innovative AI-powered applications, including chatbots and virtual assistants.

### 3.3.1 Creating Chatbots

**1 Define the Bot's Purpose**:

○ *Prompt*: "Help me design a chatbot script for a restaurant. It should handle reservations, menu inquiries, and operating hours."

**2 Develop User Flows**:

○ *Prompt*: "Create a step-by-step flowchart for a user interacting with this chatbot."

**3 Integration with APIs**:

○ ChatGPT's API capabilities can be integrated with platforms like Twilio for SMS bots or web services for live chat.

### 3.3.2 Designing Virtual Assistants

ChatGPT can assist in building personal productivity tools:

**1 Scheduling**:

○ *Prompt*: "Design a virtual assistant that integrates with Google Calendar to schedule and remind users about meetings."

**2 To-Do Lists**:

○ *Prompt*: "Generate a Python script that manages a daily to-do list with priority levels."

## 3.4 Generating Creative Works

ChatGPT's generative abilities extend into creative fields, making it a powerful tool for writers, artists, and marketers.

### 3.4.1 Writing Fiction

**1 Developing Story Ideas**:

○ *Prompt*: "Generate 5 unique story ideas in the science fiction genre."

○ Example Output:

1 A colony on Mars faces a rebellion when its AI administrator begins making unethical decisions.

2 A time traveler discovers they've inadvertently erased their own existence.

**2 Character Development**:

○ *Prompt*: "Create a detailed profile for a protagonist who is a reluctant superhero."

**3 World-Building**:

○ *Prompt*: "Describe a futuristic city where humans coexist with sentient robots. Focus on its architecture and culture."

| Idea Type | Description |
|---|---|
| Story Outlines | Generate detailed outlines for novels or scripts. |
| Character Design | Create profiles with backstories and motivations. |
| World-Building | Design fictional settings, cultures, and histories. |
| Poetry | Compose sonnets, haikus, or free verse poems. |
| Dialogues | Write engaging dialogues for plays or stories. |

*A grid of icons and short descriptions highlighting ChatGPT's potential in creative writing*

### 3.4.2 Crafting Poetry

ChatGPT can compose poems in various styles:
- *Prompt*: "Write a haiku about the beauty of a rainy day."
- *Output*:

*Silver droplets fall,*
*Nature whispers in the mist,*
*Peaceful hearts rejoice.*

### 3.4.3 Creating Ad Copy

For marketers, ChatGPT can produce persuasive ad copy:
- *Prompt*: "Write a Facebook ad promoting a new eco-friendly water bottle. Highlight its sustainability features."

**Example Output**:

"🌿 Stay hydrated, save the planet! Meet AquaPure, the reusable water bottle made from 100% recycled materials. Perfect for your adventures and kind to the Earth. 💧 Get yours today!"

## 3.5 Industry-Specific Applications

ChatGPT can also be tailored to meet the needs of specific industries. Here are some examples:

. . .

### 3.5.1 Healthcare
- **Patient FAQs**:
  - *Prompt*: "Write an FAQ for a dental clinic about common procedures."
- **Educational Materials**:
  - *Prompt*: "Create a simplified explanation of Type 2 Diabetes for patients."

### 3.5.2 Education
- **Lesson Plans**:
  - *Prompt*: "Design a week-long lesson plan for teaching basic algebra to 8th graders."
- **Quiz Generation**:
  - *Prompt*: "Create a 10-question quiz on the American Revolution for high school students."

### 3.5.3 E-Commerce
- **Product Descriptions**:
  - *Prompt*: "Write a detailed and engaging description for a luxury leather handbag."
- **Customer Support**:
  - *Prompt*: "Generate responses for a chatbot handling common order-related inquiries."

## 3.6 Enhancing Collaboration with Teams

ChatGPT is not only for solo users—it's also a valuable tool for team collaboration.

- **Meeting Summaries**:
  - *Prompt*: "Summarize the key points from this meeting transcript."
- **Brainstorming Sessions**:

○ *Prompt*: "Generate 20 taglines for a new product launch. The theme is innovation and simplicity."

**Actionable Exercises to Master ChatGPT's Potential**
  **1 Content Creation**:
  ○ Prompt: "Draft a 700-word article about how AI is transforming digital marketing."
  ○ Refine the draft by asking, "Add three case studies and a conclusion."
  **2 Coding Tasks**:
  ○ Prompt: "Write a JavaScript function that validates an email address."
  ○ Ask for an explanation: "Explain how this function works."
  **3 Creative Writing**:
  ○ Prompt: "Create a plot summary for a mystery novel set in a small coastal town."
  **4 Team Collaboration**:
  ○ Prompt: "Write an email summarizing our team's progress on the Q1 marketing strategy."

## 3.7 Prompt Templates and Libraries

Creating effective prompts is key to unlocking ChatGPT's full potential. This section provides a library of pre-designed prompt templates organized by category. These templates will save time, inspire creativity, and guide readers in crafting precise inputs for a variety of use cases.

### 3.7.1 Content Creation Templates
  **Blog Writing**
  • **Prompt**: "Write a 1,000-word blog post on [topic], targeting

[audience]. Use an [informative/casual/engaging] tone. Include an introduction, 3 main points, and a conclusion."

○ *Example*: "Write a 1,000-word blog post on 'Sustainable Living Tips' targeting environmentally conscious millennials. Use an engaging tone."

- **SEO Optimization**:

○ *Prompt*: "Generate 5 SEO-friendly headlines for a blog about [topic]. Include [keyword]."

**Social Media Content**
- **Instagram Captions**:

○ *Prompt*: "Write a catchy Instagram caption for a photo of [description]. Include a call-to-action."

○ *Example*: "Write a caption for a photo of a sunset over the ocean, promoting a travel agency."

- **LinkedIn Post**:

○ *Prompt*: "Draft a professional LinkedIn post announcing [event/achievement]. Keep it under 150 words."

**Video Scripts**
- **Prompt**: "Create a 2-minute video script for [platform] on [topic]. Include an attention-grabbing opening, 3 key points, and a closing call-to-action."

### 3.7.2 Coding and Technical Templates
**Code Generation**
- **Prompt**: "Write a [language] program to [task]. Include comments for each step."

○ *Example*: "Write a Python program to calculate compound interest. Include comments."

**Debugging**
- **Prompt**: "Find and fix errors in this code snippet: [insert code]. Explain what changes you made and why."

○ *Example*: Provide a buggy piece of code for ChatGPT to debug and demonstrate its corrections.

**Documentation**
- **Prompt**: "Generate a README file for a project that [description]. Include sections for installation, usage, and contributing."
  - *Example*: "Generate a README file for a project that scrapes data from a website and visualizes it in charts."

### 3.7.3 Business and Professional Templates
**Marketing**
- **Prompt**: "Write a persuasive email promoting [product/service]. Highlight [features/benefits] and include a call-to-action."
  - *Example*: "Write an email promoting an AI-powered project management tool. Highlight time savings and ease of use."

**Customer Service**
- **Prompt**: "Create a polite and professional response to a customer complaint about [issue]."
  - *Example*: "Respond to a customer who received a damaged product and wants a refund."

**Reports and Proposals**
- **Prompt**: "Draft a [type of document] for [purpose]. Include sections for [key elements]."
  - *Example*: "Draft a project proposal for implementing AI in customer support. Include objectives, benefits, and costs."

### 3.7.4 Creative Writing Templates
**Story Development**
- **Prompt**: "Create a story outline for a [genre] story. The main character is [description], and the central conflict is [conflict]."
  - *Example*: "Create a story outline for a fantasy novel. The main character is a young wizard who must uncover a conspiracy to overthrow the kingdom."

**Character Design**

- **Prompt**: "Generate a detailed profile for a [role]. Include their background, personality traits, and motivations."
- ○ *Example*: "Generate a detailed profile for a detective in a crime thriller."

**Poetry**
- **Prompt**: "Write a [form of poetry, e.g., haiku, sonnet] about [theme]."
- ○ *Example*: "Write a haiku about the serenity of a forest."

### 3.7.5 Industry-Specific Templates

**Healthcare**
- **Prompt**: "Simplify this medical concept: [concept]. Make it understandable to a non-expert."
- ○ *Example*: "Simplify the concept of 'hypertension' for a general audience."
- **Patient Education**:
- ○ *Prompt*: "Write a patient guide explaining [procedure/condition]. Keep it clear and empathetic."

**Education**
- **Lesson Planning**:
- ○ *Prompt*: "Design a week-long lesson plan for teaching [subject] to [grade level]. Include objectives, activities, and materials."
- ○ *Example*: "Design a week-long lesson plan for teaching photosynthesis to 7th graders."
- **Quiz Creation**:
- ○ *Prompt*: "Generate a 10-question quiz on [topic]. Include multiple-choice and short-answer questions."
- ○ *Example*: "Generate a 10-question quiz on the American Revolution."

**E-Commerce**
- **Product Descriptions**:
- ○ *Prompt*: "Write an engaging product description for [item]. Highlight [features]."

o *Example*: "Write a product description for a luxury leather wallet, highlighting its craftsmanship and durability."
- **Ad Copy**:
o *Prompt*: "Create a Google Ad for [product/service]. Include a headline, description, and call-to-action."

| Domain | Use Case | Example Prompt |
|---|---|---|
| Content Creation | Writing blog posts, scripts | "Write a 1,000-word blog on AI in healthcare." |
| Coding & Development | Debugging and optimizing code | "Fix this Python script and explain your changes." |
| Marketing | Ad copy and email campaigns | "Create an email promoting our new AI software." |
| Education | Lesson plans, quizzes, and simplifications | "Generate a week-long lesson on photosynthesis." |
| Creative Writing | Story outlines, poetry, and character design | "Outline a sci-fi story about time travel." |

*A table summarizing applications of ChatGPT across industries*

### 3.7.6 Personal Productivity Templates
**Time Management**
- **Prompt**: "Create a weekly schedule for someone balancing [tasks]. Include time for [specific activities]."

o *Example*: "Create a weekly schedule for someone working remotely, exercising, and learning a new skill."

**Goal Setting**
- **Prompt**: "Help me create a SMART goal for [objective]."

o *Example*: "Help me create a SMART goal for launching a blog in three months."

**Life Planning**
- **Prompt**: "Suggest a step-by-step plan for achieving [personal goal]."

o *Example*: "Suggest a step-by-step plan for saving for a down payment on a house."

## Pro Tips for Using Templates
### 1 Customize to Fit Your Needs:
o Templates are starting points. Add your unique context or requirements for better results.
### 2 Experiment with Tone and Style:
o Modify prompts to suit formal, casual, or humorous tones depending on your audience.
### 3 Iterate and Refine:
o Use follow-up prompts to build on the initial output and improve quality.

# Troubleshooting Common Challenges

As powerful as ChatGPT is, users may sometimes encounter challenges while using it. These challenges typically stem from unclear prompts, misunderstandings of ChatGPT's capabilities, or the inherent limitations of generative AI. Understanding these challenges—and how to overcome them—will ensure a smoother and more productive experience.

### Common Challenges and Solutions
### 1. Receiving Generic or Vague Responses
**Problem**: ChatGPT produces overly general answers that lack depth or relevance.

**Why It Happens**:
• The prompt is too broad or unclear.
• There is insufficient context for ChatGPT to tailor the response.

**Solution**:
• Add specificity and constraints to your prompt.

• Include details about the purpose, audience, tone, and format of the response.

• Use follow-up prompts to refine and narrow the scope.

**Example**:

• *Weak Prompt*: "Write about AI."

• *Improved Prompt*: "Write a 500-word article about how AI is transforming small businesses, focusing on marketing automation and cost reduction."

## 2. Incorrect or Inaccurate Information

**Problem**: ChatGPT occasionally generates outputs that are factually incorrect or outdated.

**Why It Happens**:

• ChatGPT is a language model trained on data up to a specific cutoff (currently 2021) and may not access real-time or specialized knowledge.

• It might infer plausible-sounding, but incorrect, information.

**Solution**:

• **Verify and Cross-Check**: Always validate critical or technical information against reliable sources.

• **Explicitly Ask for Caveats**: Request disclaimers or uncertainties in the response.

  o *Prompt*: "Provide this information with a note on its accuracy and potential limitations."

**Example**:

• *Original Output*: "Mars is closer to Earth than Venus."

• *Follow-Up Prompt*: "Double-check and clarify this fact with distances in miles."

## 3. Misunderstanding Complex Prompts

**Problem**: ChatGPT struggles to interpret or respond accurately to overly complex or layered instructions.

**Why It Happens**:
• The prompt is too detailed or combines unrelated queries.
• ChatGPT loses focus when presented with multi-part instructions in one query.

**Solution**:
• Break the task into smaller, focused steps.
• Use iterative refinement to build upon previous responses.

**Example**:
• *Overwhelming Prompt*: "Write a 1,000-word blog on AI in healthcare, include examples, statistics, and explain ethical challenges."
• *Improved Workflow*:
1 Start with: "Outline a blog on AI in healthcare, listing key sections."
2 Then: "Expand the section on ethical challenges with examples and statistics."
3 Lastly: "Combine the responses into a cohesive draft."

## 4. Responses Lacking Creativity or Originality

**Problem**: The output feels repetitive, uninspired, or too similar to common knowledge.

**Why It Happens**:
• The model defaults to generic patterns if the prompt doesn't encourage originality.
• It avoids risks, preferring safer, well-known ideas.

**Solution**:
• Push ChatGPT to "think outside the box" by framing the prompt with creative constraints or asking for unique perspectives.
• Use role-based prompting to introduce novelty.
  o *Prompt*: "Act as a science-fiction writer and describe a world where AI governs cities."

. . .

## 5. Overly Long or Rambling Responses

**Problem**: ChatGPT generates lengthy, unfocused answers.

**Why It Happens**:

• The prompt doesn't specify a word limit or desired level of detail.

• ChatGPT tries to cover all possible angles to ensure relevance.

**Solution**:

• Define constraints upfront, such as word count or key points to focus on.

• Use feedback to shorten and streamline responses.

  ○ *Prompt*: "Summarize this in 3 bullet points."


## 6. Difficulty Handling Industry-Specific Jargon

**Problem**: ChatGPT struggles with highly technical or niche terminology.

**Why It Happens**:

• The language model isn't deeply specialized in certain fields.

• The prompt doesn't provide enough context for interpretation.

**Solution**:

• Offer definitions or context for specialized terms.

  ○ *Prompt*: "Using layman's terms, explain quantum entanglement in the context of computing."

• Ask for simplified or tiered explanations.

  ○ *Prompt*: "Explain this legal term first to a beginner and then in professional detail."

## General Tips for Troubleshooting

**1 Rephrase and Retry**:
- If ChatGPT misunderstands your query, rephrase the prompt using simpler language or a different structure.
- Example: Instead of "Generate a framework for agile project management," try "List the key principles of agile project management and explain each."

**2 Use Feedback Loops**:
- Guide ChatGPT by asking it to refine or improve its initial output.
- Example: "This response is too formal. Make it conversational and engaging."

**3 Recognize Limitations**:
- ChatGPT is not a search engine or a specialist—its strength lies in generating plausible language, not verified facts. Use it as a starting point, not a definitive source.

**4 Leverage Prompt Templates**:
- Use pre-tested prompt structures for specific use cases, such as:
  - "Summarize this article in 100 words."
  - "Generate 5 ideas for marketing a new fitness app."

**5 Seek External Support**:
- For complex projects, combine ChatGPT with other tools (e.g., Grammarly for editing or Google for fact-checking).

. . .

**Conclusion**

ChatGPT's potential is vast, spanning content creation, coding, application development, and creative pursuits. By experimenting with different use cases and refining your prompts, you can unlock new levels of productivity and creativity.

In the next chapter, we'll delve into the art of monetizing ChatGPT, exploring practical strategies to turn its capabilities into income streams. Get ready to transform skills into profits!

# Chapter 4
# Comprehensive Strategies for Income Generation

ChatGPT is more than just a tool—it's a gateway to profitable opportunities. With its versatile capabilities, individuals and businesses can transform ChatGPT's outputs into valuable income streams. This chapter dives deeper into monetization strategies, providing detailed examples, actionable steps, and advanced techniques to help you turn ChatGPT into a powerful asset for making money online.

## 4.1 Offering Freelance Writing and Content Services

Freelance writing is one of the most accessible ways to monetize ChatGPT. With its ability to generate articles, ad copy, and technical documents, ChatGPT can help you meet the demands of clients across industries.

### 4.1.1 Identifying Your Writing Niche

Focus on areas where ChatGPT's assistance aligns with your interests or expertise:

- **SEO Blog Writing**: Target businesses looking for search-engine-optimized content.

- **Technical Writing**: Use ChatGPT to simplify complex concepts.
- **Copywriting**: Create compelling sales copy for products or services.

**Example**:
- *Niche*: Fitness and wellness content.
- *Prompt*: "Write a 1,200-word blog post on the benefits of HIIT workouts for beginners. Include tips, benefits, and a sample workout plan."

### 4.1.2 Attracting Clients
**1 Portfolio Creation**:
- Use ChatGPT to draft professional-quality writing samples for your portfolio.
- *Example*: "Write an engaging product description for a smart home security camera."

**2 Marketing Yourself**:
- Use LinkedIn or freelance platforms like Fiverr, Upwork, and Freelancer to promote your services.
- *Prompt*: "Write a LinkedIn summary for a freelance content writer specializing in AI-assisted blog writing."

### 4.1.3 Maximizing Efficiency
ChatGPT speeds up your workflow:

**1 Draft Creation**:
- Generate a rough draft and edit manually to match client requirements.

**2 Bulk Content Creation**:
- Offer packages like "10 blog posts per month" by leveraging ChatGPT's quick output capabilities.

**Pro Tip**: Charge based on the value delivered, not the time spent. Use ChatGPT's speed to your advantage without undervaluing your work.

## 4.2 AI-Driven Digital Marketing: Unlocking Opportunities

Digital marketing is an essential part of modern business. ChatGPT allows you to offer cutting-edge marketing services at a fraction of the traditional effort.

### 4.2.1 Key Digital Marketing Services

- **Ad Campaign Creation**: Design attention-grabbing Google, Facebook, or Instagram ads.
- **Email Marketing**: Write high-conversion email sequences.
- **Social Media Management**: Create content calendars and engaging posts.

**Example**:

- *Prompt*: "Write a 5-step email sequence for a skincare brand promoting a new anti-aging serum. Each email should build excitement and encourage purchases."

### 4.2.2 Running a Social Media Management Business

**1 Content Creation**:

  o Generate captions, hashtags, and post ideas using ChatGPT.
  o *Prompt*: "Write 10 Instagram captions for a travel agency promoting adventure tours."

**2 Analytics Reports**:

  o Pair ChatGPT with tools like Google Analytics to create client reports.
  o *Prompt*: "Summarize this website traffic data into actionable recommendations."

**Advanced Example**: Offer AI-assisted branding consultations:

- *Prompt*: "Suggest a unique brand voice for a sustainable clothing line targeting Gen Z."

## 4.3 Creating and Selling Digital Products

Digital products such as e-books, online courses, and templates are scalable income streams that ChatGPT can help you create efficiently.

### 4.3.1 Writing E-Books

**1 Identify a Profitable Topic**:
- Use ChatGPT to brainstorm ideas.
- *Prompt*: "List 10 e-book topics for aspiring entrepreneurs in 2024."

**2 Create the Content**:
- Use ChatGPT to generate chapter outlines, introductions, and content.
- *Prompt*: "Write the introduction for an e-book titled 'Mastering Freelance Success.'"

**3 Publish and Promote**:
- Use platforms like Amazon Kindle Direct Publishing or Gumroad to sell your e-book.
- *Prompt*: "Write a promotional email for my e-book on time management."

### 4.3.2 Building Online Courses

**1 Generate Course Outlines**:
- *Prompt*: "Create a 10-module course outline for 'Introduction to Social Media Marketing.'"

**2 Develop Materials**:
- Use ChatGPT to write course descriptions, lesson summaries, and quizzes.
- *Prompt*: "Write a quiz with 10 questions on the basics of SEO."

**3 Choose a Platform**:

○ Upload your course to Teachable, Thinkific, or Udemy.
**Pro Tip**: Bundle e-books and courses for higher-value offers.

## 4.4 Affiliate Marketing and SEO Optimization

Affiliate marketing involves promoting products or services and earning a commission for each sale or lead generated. ChatGPT streamlines content creation for affiliate websites and blogs.

### 4.4.1 Building an Affiliate Marketing Blog

**1 Select a Profitable Niche**:
  ○ *Prompt*: "Suggest profitable affiliate marketing niches for 2024. Focus on underserved markets."

**2 Write High-Quality Content**:
  ○ Create product reviews, comparisons, and guides.
  ○ *Prompt*: "Write a detailed product review comparing the top 3 smartwatches for fitness enthusiasts."

**3 SEO-Optimized Posts**:
  ○ Generate keyword-rich headlines and meta descriptions.
  ○ *Prompt*: "Suggest 5 SEO-friendly blog titles about eco-friendly kitchen appliances."

### 4.4.2 Diversifying Income Streams

  • **Email Newsletters**:
  ○ *Prompt*: "Write a weekly newsletter introducing eco-friendly gadgets with affiliate links."
  • **Social Media Campaigns**:
  ○ Use ChatGPT to create Instagram posts and ads promoting affiliate products.

## 4.5 Scaling E-Commerce with ChatGPT

ChatGPT can transform your e-commerce business by automating essential tasks, improving customer experiences, and boosting sales.

### 4.5.1 Writing Product Descriptions
**1 Craft Compelling Descriptions**:
- *Prompt*: "Write a detailed, engaging product description for a noise-canceling wireless headphone."

**2 Tailor for Different Platforms**:
- *Prompt*: "Rewrite this product description to fit Amazon's tone and guidelines."

### 4.5.2 Enhancing Customer Engagement
- **Automated Chatbots**:
  - *Prompt*: "Create chatbot responses for an e-commerce site. Include responses for shipping delays, returns, and product inquiries."
- **Email Campaigns**:
  - *Prompt*: "Write a 3-part email series for a flash sale on fitness equipment."

## 4.6 Combining ChatGPT with Automation and APIs

By integrating ChatGPT with automation tools and APIs, you can scale operations efficiently and create innovative AI-powered services.

### 4.6.1 Automating Workflows
- Pair ChatGPT with tools like Zapier or Integromat to automate:
  - Generating daily content.
  - Sending automated email responses.
- *Example*: Automate blog posting by generating drafts with ChatGPT and uploading them via WordPress integrations.

### 4.6.2 Developing AI-Powered Subscriptions

Offer recurring services powered by ChatGPT:

**1 Content Subscriptions**:
o Provide weekly blog posts, social media captions, or newsletters.
o *Prompt*: "Generate 5 weekly blog topics for a tech startup."

**2 Personalized Coaching Tools**:
o Use ChatGPT to provide templates for personalized advice.
o *Prompt*: "Create a productivity plan for someone balancing work and studying."

## 4.7 Advanced Monetization Strategies

### 4.7.1 Hosting Workshops or Webinars

Teach others how to use ChatGPT effectively:
• *Prompt*: "Write a workshop agenda for 'How to Use ChatGPT to Start a Freelance Business.'"

### 4.7.2 Creating Niche AI Services

Offer specialized AI services in areas like:

• **Grant Writing**:
o *Prompt*: "Draft a grant proposal for a community literacy project."

• **Legal Drafting**:
o *Prompt*: "Write a simple service agreement for a freelance graphic designer."

## 4.8 Ethical Considerations for Monetization

### 4.8.1 Ensuring Originality

• Always refine and personalize AI-generated content to add

value and avoid plagiarism.

### 4.8.2 Transparency with Clients

• Clearly communicate when and how you've used ChatGPT in your work.

### 4.8.3 Responsible Use of Data

• Avoid feeding sensitive or confidential information into ChatGPT.

## Conclusion

ChatGPT's potential for monetization is virtually limitless. By exploring freelancing, digital marketing, e-commerce, and automation, you can turn ChatGPT into a reliable source of income. In the next chapter, we'll explore **advanced AI integrations**, diving deeper into automation tools, APIs, and other technologies to scale and diversify your ChatGPT-powered ventures. The possibilities are only beginning!

# Chapter 5
# Advanced AI Integration for Profit

In this chapter, we'll explore how to combine ChatGPT with automation tools, APIs, and other AI-driven technologies to streamline workflows, enhance scalability, and create innovative, profitable services. By integrating ChatGPT into advanced setups, you can achieve higher efficiency, serve more clients, and unlock new revenue streams.

## 5.1 Automating Workflows for Efficiency and Scalability

Automation is essential for scaling any business. Combining ChatGPT with tools like **Zapier**, **Make (formerly Integromat)**, or **IFTTT** can help you automate repetitive tasks, freeing up time for higher-value work.

### 5.1.1 Workflow Automation Basics

Automation tools act as a bridge between apps and services, enabling tasks to run seamlessly without manual intervention.

**Example: Automating Content Creation and Publishing**

**1 Idea Generation:**

○ Use ChatGPT to brainstorm ideas.

○ *Prompt*: "Suggest 10 blog post topics for a wellness brand."

**2 Content Drafting:**

○ Automate draft creation by connecting ChatGPT to Google Docs.

**3 Publishing:**

○ Use Zapier to automatically post the draft to WordPress or social media platforms.

**Step-by-Step Guide to Automating Blog Posting**

**1 Connect ChatGPT via API:**

○ Use OpenAI's API to integrate ChatGPT into your content workflow.

**2 Create a Zap (Zapier):**

○ Trigger: New Google Sheet row with blog topics.

○ Action: Generate content using ChatGPT and save it to Google Docs.

○ Final Action: Publish the content to WordPress.

**5.1.2 Automating Customer Communication**

ChatGPT can automate email responses, FAQs, and chatbot conversations:

• **Email Support:**

○ Use ChatGPT to generate personalized replies based on customer queries.

○ *Prompt*: "Write a polite response to a customer asking about a refund for a damaged product."

• **Chatbots:**

○ Integrate ChatGPT with platforms like **Twilio** or **Dialogflow** to create intelligent chatbots.

**Example: E-Commerce Customer Support Automation**

**1 Trigger**: Customer submits a support query via the website.

**2 Action**: ChatGPT generates a response based on the query type.

**3 Output**: Automated email or chatbot reply is sent to the customer.

## 5.2 Combining ChatGPT with APIs

ChatGPT's API allows developers to integrate its capabilities directly into applications, creating custom solutions for various industries.

### 5.2.1 What is an API?

An API (Application Programming Interface) allows two software systems to communicate with each other. ChatGPT's API enables developers to send prompts and receive responses programmatically.

### 5.2.2 Practical Applications of ChatGPT APIs

**1 Custom Chatbots**:

○ Build chatbots tailored for specific industries like healthcare, education, or real estate.

○ *Example*: A real estate chatbot that answers FAQs about property listings.

**2 AI-Powered Tools**:

○ Integrate ChatGPT into SaaS platforms for content generation, data analysis, or customer interactions.

○ *Example*: A tool that generates personalized workout plans for fitness app users.

**3 Data Analysis**:

○ Use ChatGPT to analyze survey responses or summarize large datasets.

### 5.2.3 How to Get Started with ChatGPT's API
**1 Sign Up for API Access**:
○ Visit OpenAI's website to obtain API keys.
**2 Choose a Programming Language**:
○ Python is commonly used for API integration.
**3 Build and Test**:
• Write scripts to send prompts and process responses.
• *Example Code*:

```python
import openai

openai.api_key = "your-api-key"

response = openai.Completion.create(
    engine="text-davinci-003",
    prompt="Generate a blog outline for AI in education",
    max_tokens=150
)

print(response.choices[0].text.strip())
```

**4 Deploy Your Application**:
○ Host your solution on a cloud platform like AWS or Google Cloud.

. . .

## 5.3 Creating Subscription-Based Services Powered by AI

Subscription models provide predictable revenue streams and are well-suited for AI-powered offerings.

### 5.3.1 AI Content Subscriptions

Offer content creation as a subscription service:

**1 Weekly Blog Posts**:

o Create a package for businesses where ChatGPT generates SEO-optimized blogs every week.

o *Example*: "$500/month for four high-quality blog posts tailored to your business."

**2 Social Media Packages**:

o Automate weekly captions, hashtags, and post ideas.

o *Prompt*: "Generate 10 Instagram captions for a boutique clothing brand targeting millennials."

### 5.3.2 Personalized AI Services

Develop subscription services tailored to individual users:

- **Fitness Plans**:

o *Prompt*: "Create a 4-week workout plan for a beginner with weight loss goals."

- **Study Guides**:

o *Prompt*: "Generate a personalized study plan for a student preparing for the SAT."

### 5.3.3 API-Driven Tools for Clients

Offer subscription-based access to custom AI tools:

- **Example**: A SaaS product that generates custom marketing plans.
- **Revenue Model**: Charge monthly or yearly fees for access.

## 5.4 Using AI Insights for Business Analytics

ChatGPT can analyze and interpret data, making it a valuable tool for business decision-making.

### 5.4.1 Turning Data into Insights
**1 Summarize Reports**:
- *Prompt*: "Summarize this financial report in 200 words, focusing on key trends."

**2 Analyze Customer Feedback**:
- Use ChatGPT to identify patterns in survey responses or reviews.
- *Prompt*: "Analyze this customer feedback and provide 3 key themes."

### 5.4.2 Scenario Planning
Simulate business scenarios to evaluate decisions:
- *Prompt*: "What are the pros and cons of opening a second location for a coffee shop in a new city?"

## 5.5 Innovative AI-Driven Business Models

### 5.5.1 AI-Assisted Market Research
Help businesses understand market trends using ChatGPT:

**1 Industry Analysis**:
- *Prompt*: "Analyze emerging trends in the renewable energy sector and suggest opportunities for startups."

**2 Competitor Insights**:
- *Prompt*: "List the strengths and weaknesses of [Competitor] based on public reviews and market reports."

### 5.5.2 Educational Platforms
Create AI-driven learning platforms:

**1 AI Tutors:**
- Develop chatbots that provide instant answers and explanations to students.

**2 Customized Study Materials:**
- *Prompt*: "Create a detailed study guide for the French Revolution for high school students."

### 5.5.3 Personalized E-Commerce Recommendations

Use ChatGPT to suggest products based on customer preferences:
- *Prompt*: "Based on this purchase history, suggest 5 related products for a personalized email."

## 5.6 Ethical Considerations in Advanced AI Use

### 5.6.1 Transparency
- Clearly disclose to clients or users when AI has been used to generate outputs.

### 5.6.2 Data Privacy
- Avoid inputting sensitive or personal information into ChatGPT.

### 5.6.3 Quality Assurance
- Always review AI-generated outputs to ensure accuracy and appropriateness.

## 5.7 Real-World Success Stories

**1 Automated E-Commerce Chatbots:**
- A Shopify store owner reduced customer service costs by 70% by implementing a ChatGPT-powered chatbot.

**2 AI Marketing Agency:**
- A freelancer scaled their business by combining ChatGPT

with automation tools to deliver content packages for multiple clients.

**3 Custom SaaS Platform:**
- A tech entrepreneur built an AI-driven platform that generates business proposals for startups, charging users $50/month.

**Conclusion and Next Steps**

Integrating ChatGPT with automation tools, APIs, and advanced business models unlocks incredible opportunities for scaling and innovation. By building custom solutions, automating workflows, and leveraging AI insights, you can create unique, profitable ventures. In the next chapter, we'll explore the art of prompt optimization, offering a library of prompts to help you tailor ChatGPT's outputs for maximum impact in any niche or industry.

## Chapter 6
# Unlocking the Hidden Power of Prompts

## Prompts for Every Niche

Prompts are the secret sauce to extracting the best outputs from ChatGPT. In this section, we provide over 150 tailored prompts across various niches, offering you actionable examples to jumpstart creativity, problem-solving, and innovation. Use these prompts as they are, or adapt them to suit your specific needs.

## 6.1 Content Creation

- **6.1.1 Blog Post Outlines**
  - 1 "Create an outline for a blog post on the benefits of mindfulness meditation for busy professionals."
  - 2 "Generate a detailed outline for a blog titled 'Top 10 Trends in Digital Marketing for 2024.'"
  - 3 "Write a blog outline explaining how AI is transforming the education sector."

- 4 *"Create a step-by-step guide on how to start a small online business."*
- 5 *"Generate 5 blog post ideas for a fitness and wellness blog."*
- **6.1.2 Persuasive Emails**
- 1 *"Draft a persuasive email to potential clients, introducing my freelance web design services."*
- 2 *"Write a follow-up email thanking a customer for their recent purchase and offering a discount for their next order."*
- 3 *"Compose an email to a CEO, pitching a collaboration opportunity for a green tech initiative."*
- 4 *"Write a professional cold email to a brand ambassador for a partnership."*
- 5 *"Create a welcome email for new subscribers to an online fashion newsletter."*
- **6.1.3 Ad Copy**
- 1 *"Write a Facebook ad promoting a meal subscription service, focusing on convenience and healthy eating."*
- 2 *"Create a Google Ad for an eco-friendly laundry detergent. Highlight sustainability and cost savings."*
- 3 *"Draft an Instagram caption for a luxury watch brand. Make it aspirational and sleek."*
- 4 *"Write a YouTube ad script for an AI-powered project management tool."*
- 5 *"Generate 3 ad copy variations for a limited-time sale on fitness equipment."*

# 6.2 Coding

- **6.2.1 Solving Algorithms**
- 1 *"Write a Python program to find the nth Fibonacci number."*

- 2 *"Solve the traveling salesman problem using a genetic algorithm in Python."*
- 3 *"Explain how to implement binary search in JavaScript with a code example."*
- 4 *"Generate a SQL query to find the second-highest salary in an employee table."*
- 5 *"Create a function in C++ to check if a string is a palindrome."*
- **6.2.2 Tutorials and Explanations**
- 1 *"Write a beginner-friendly tutorial on how to set up a React.js project."*
- 2 *"Explain the difference between REST and GraphQL with examples."*
- 3 *"Create a guide for deploying a Flask app on AWS Lambda."*
- 4 *"Explain recursion in programming using Python examples."*
- 5 *"Write a step-by-step guide to building a basic chatbot using Python."*
- **6.2.3 Debugging**
- 1 *"Debug this JavaScript code for calculating the factorial of a number: [code]."*
- 2 *"Fix the error in this SQL query for updating records: [code]."*
- 3 *"Optimize this Python script for faster execution: [code]."*
- 4 *"Find the bug in this Java code for sorting an array: [code]."*
- 5 *"Rewrite this PHP code snippet to improve security against SQL injection: [code]."*

## 6.3 Marketing

- **6.3.1 Social Media Strategies**
- *1 "Create a 5-post content plan for an Instagram account promoting handmade candles."*
- *2 "Generate 10 caption ideas for a fitness influencer launching a new training program."*
- *3 "Suggest hashtags for a skincare brand targeting Gen Z customers."*
- *4 "Write a week-long content calendar for a YouTube channel focused on gaming."*
- *5 "Outline a LinkedIn strategy to promote a leadership coaching business."*
- **6.3.2 Viral Campaign Ideas**
- *1 "Propose a viral TikTok campaign for a coffee shop's grand opening."*
- *2 "Generate 3 creative ideas for a giveaway contest for an online fashion retailer."*
- *3 "Design a shareable social media challenge for a fitness app."*
- *4 "Outline a Twitter thread campaign explaining the benefits of electric vehicles."*
- *5 "Suggest a theme for an influencer marketing campaign promoting an eco-tourism destination."*
- **6.3.3 General Marketing Plans**
- *1 "Create a 6-month digital marketing plan for a new SaaS product."*
- *2 "Outline a holiday marketing campaign for a small bakery."*
- *3 "Generate ideas for a cross-promotion between a local gym and a smoothie bar."*
- *4 "Design a promotional strategy for a mobile app launch."*

- 5 "Suggest a loyalty program structure for a subscription-based streaming service."

## 6.4 Personal Productivity

- **6.4.1 Life Hacks**
- 1 "List 10 productivity hacks for remote workers."
- 2 "Generate a daily routine for someone balancing a full-time job and online learning."
- 3 "Suggest strategies for managing email overload effectively."
- 4 "Write a step-by-step guide to decluttering a home office."
- 5 "Recommend apps and tools for improving time management."
- **6.4.2 Brainstorming**
- 1 "Suggest unique side hustle ideas for someone skilled in graphic design."
- 2 "Brainstorm 10 ideas for an eco-friendly startup."
- 3 "List hobbies for someone who wants to develop creative skills."
- 4 "Generate innovative ideas for celebrating a virtual team-building event."
- 5 "Propose 5 unique themes for a small dinner party."
- **6.4.3 Learning Plans**
- 1 "Create a 30-day learning plan to master basic Python programming."
- 2 "Design a weekly study schedule for preparing for the GRE."
- 3 "Suggest resources and a plan for learning French in 6 months."
- 4 "Outline a personal development plan for improving leadership skills."

- 5 "Generate a step-by-step guide to learning how to play the guitar."

## 6.5 Business Growth

- **6.5.1 Financial Modeling**
- 1 "Create a basic financial model for a subscription-based business."
- 2 "Explain how to calculate the break-even point for a small bakery."
- 3 "Generate a 12-month profit projection for an e-commerce store selling fitness gear."
- 4 "Write a step-by-step guide to calculating customer lifetime value (CLV)."
- 5 "Create a financial template for tracking monthly expenses and revenue."
- **6.5.2 Customer Support Scripts**
- 1 "Write a polite response to a customer requesting a refund for late delivery."
- 2 "Generate a chatbot script for an online bookstore handling common queries."
- 3 "Draft a response to a negative customer review about a restaurant's service."
- 4 "Create an email template for following up with inactive customers."
- 5 "Write a script for handling customer complaints about defective products."
- **6.5.3 Strategic Planning**
- 1 "Outline a 5-year growth strategy for a boutique clothing brand."
- 2 "Suggest strategies for entering a new international market for a tech startup."

- 3 *"Propose a framework for scaling a local bakery into a franchise."*
- 4 *"Generate a SWOT analysis for a new subscription box service."*
- 5 *"Design a roadmap for launching an AI-powered customer service platform."*

## Unique and Unexpected Ideas for Using ChatGPT

ChatGPT isn't just a tool for conventional tasks—it's a creative powerhouse capable of opening new and unexpected doors for unique projects and income streams. This section of Chapter 6 dives into innovative applications such as writing children's books, designing board games, crafting personalized greeting cards, creating online quizzes, and offering niche AI-driven services like grant writing. These ideas are actionable, scalable, and designed to inspire you to think outside the box.

### 6.6 Writing Children's Books with Illustrated Story Prompts

Children's books are an evergreen market with consistent demand, and ChatGPT can help streamline the creative process by generating imaginative stories, engaging characters, and age-appropriate language.

#### 6.6.1 How ChatGPT Can Help
**1 Generate Story Ideas**:
  o *Prompt*: "Suggest five unique story ideas for children aged 5–8 that include an animal protagonist and a moral lesson."
  o Example Output:
  1 *The Brave Little Hedgehog*: A story about overcoming fear.
  2 *Ellie the Eco-Elephant*: Teaching kids the value of recycling.

**2 Create Detailed Storylines**:

○ *Prompt*: "Outline a children's story about a magical tree that grants wishes, but only to those with kind hearts."

**3 Character Development**:
○ *Prompt*: "Describe a lovable talking dog character for a children's book. Include personality traits and quirks."

**4 Write the Story**:
○ *Prompt*: "Write a 1,000-word children's story about a boy who discovers he can talk to clouds."

**6.6.2 Pairing with Illustrators**

Once the story is written, pair the text with illustrations:

**1 Collaborate with Artists**:
○ Use freelance platforms like Fiverr or Upwork to find illustrators.

**2 AI Art Generators**:
○ Use AI tools like DALL·E to create preliminary illustrations based on your story prompts.

**6.6.3 Monetizing Children's Books**

**1 Self-Publish**:
○ Platforms like Amazon Kindle Direct Publishing (KDP) or Lulu allow you to publish e-books or print-on-demand paperbacks.

**2 Create Bundles**:
○ Offer themed series (e.g., "Adventures of the Eco Heroes") to attract repeat buyers.

**3 Market to Schools**:
○ Approach schools or libraries with educational stories aligned with classroom themes.

## 6.7 Designing Board Games and Escape Room Narratives

Board games and escape rooms thrive on creativity and storytelling, making them an exciting niche for ChatGPT applications.

### 6.7.1 Developing Board Game Concepts

**1 Theme and Mechanics:**

- *Prompt*: "Design a family-friendly board game where players build their own magical kingdoms. Include rules and winning conditions."
- Example Output:
  - Theme: Magical kingdom-building.
  - Mechanics: Collect resources, expand territories, and fend off mythical creatures.

**2 Character Cards and Gameplay Elements:**

- *Prompt*: "Create 10 unique character cards for a sci-fi-themed board game. Include their abilities and backstories."

**3 Testing and Refinement:**

- Use ChatGPT to brainstorm additional scenarios or refine rules.
- *Prompt*: "Simplify these board game rules for beginners."

### 6.7.2 Crafting Escape Room Narratives

Escape rooms thrive on engaging stories and creative puzzles:

**1 Design the Plot:**

- *Prompt*: "Write a story for an escape room set in a haunted library. Include 5 puzzles the players must solve to escape."
- Example:
  - Puzzle 1: A riddle hidden in an ancient book.
  - Puzzle 2: Decoding a message written in invisible ink.

**2 Integrate Clues and Challenges:**

- *Prompt*: "Create a cipher puzzle for an escape room where the answer is the name of a famous author."

### 3 Script NPC Interactions:
- *Prompt*: "Write dialogue for a mysterious librarian NPC who provides cryptic hints to players."

### 6.7.3 Monetizing Board Games and Escape Room Designs
#### 1 Pitch Ideas to Publishers:
- Submit your game designs to companies like Hasbro or Ravensburger.

#### 2 Sell Print-and-Play Games:
- Use platforms like Itch.io or Gumroad to sell downloadable PDFs of your board games.

#### 3 Offer Custom Escape Room Designs:
- Market your services to event planners or local businesses looking for unique team-building activities.

## 6.8 Creating Personalized Greeting Card Messages for Sale

Greeting cards are a timeless way to connect emotionally, and ChatGPT can help you craft unique, personalized messages for any occasion.

### 6.8.1 Crafting Custom Messages
#### 1 Generate Messages by Theme:
- *Prompt*: "Write a heartfelt message for a Mother's Day card."
- Example Output:

*"Mom, your love is the guiding light that makes my days brighter. Thank you for always being there. Happy Mother's Day!"*

#### 2 Unique Celebratory Cards:
- *Prompt*: "Write a funny birthday card message for someone who loves puns."

#### 3 Niche Occasions:

o *Prompt*: "Create a sympathy card message for someone grieving the loss of a pet."

### 6.8.2 Designing the Cards
Pair messages with designs:
**1 Collaborate with Graphic Designers**:
o Partner with artists to create card templates.
**2 Use Design Tools**:
o Platforms like Canva make it easy to design and print cards.

### 6.8.3 Selling Greeting Cards
**1 Etsy Stores**:
o Sell personalized cards on Etsy, offering customization options.
**2 Print-on-Demand Services**:
o Use services like Zazzle or Redbubble to sell cards without managing inventory.
**3 Social Media Promotion**:
o Share your card designs and witty messages on platforms like Instagram or Pinterest to attract buyers.

## 6.9 Generating Engaging Online Quizzes and Trivia

Quizzes and trivia games are excellent for engaging audiences online, whether for entertainment or education.

### 6.9.1 Crafting Quiz Questions
**1 Themed Trivia Quizzes**:
o *Prompt*: "Create 10 trivia questions about famous landmarks around the world."
**2 Personality Quizzes**:
o *Prompt*: "Write a personality quiz titled 'What Type of Leader Are You?' with 5 questions and results."
**3 Educational Quizzes**:

o *Prompt*: "Generate a quiz for high school students about the causes and effects of World War II."

### 6.9.2 Quiz Formats
**1 Multiple Choice**:
o *Prompt*: "Write a multiple-choice question about the history of the internet with four possible answers."
**2 True or False**:
o *Prompt*: "Create 5 true-or-false questions about the solar system."

### 6.9.3 Platforms for Publishing Quizzes
**1 Buzzfeed-Style Quizzes**:
o Use platforms like Buzzfeed or Playbuzz to share fun personality quizzes.
**2 Educational Platforms**:
o Publish quizzes on platforms like Kahoot or Quizlet for teachers and students.
**3 Monetization**:
o Offer quizzes as lead magnets to collect emails for digital marketing campaigns.

## 6.10 Offering Niche AI Services Like Grant Writing or Legal Drafts

Specialized services like grant writing and legal document drafting are high-value offerings where ChatGPT can save time and effort.

### 6.10.1 Grant Writing
**1 Generate Grant Proposals**:
o *Prompt*: "Draft a grant proposal for a non-profit organization focused on wildlife conservation."
**2 Refine and Personalize**:

o Use ChatGPT to refine drafts based on specific funding requirements.
   **3 Market Your Services**:
   o Advertise on freelance platforms or approach non-profits directly.

### 6.10.2 Legal Document Drafting
   **1 Create Templates**:
   o *Prompt*: "Draft a simple freelance contract for graphic design services."
   **2 Client-Specific Customization**:
   o *Prompt*: "Write a privacy policy for a small e-commerce website."

### 6.10.3 Monetizing Niche Services
   **1 Subscription Packages**:
   o Offer monthly subscriptions for grant or legal document writing.
   **2 Consulting**:
   o Use ChatGPT to assist clients in understanding and creating complex documents.

These unique and unexpected applications showcase ChatGPT's creative potential beyond traditional uses. From crafting children's stories and designing board games to creating quizzes and offering specialized services, the possibilities are limitless. By thinking outside the box and leveraging ChatGPT in these niches, you can tap into new markets and develop innovative revenue streams.

# Tips You've Never Thought Of: Leveraging ChatGPT for Unique Opportunities

ChatGPT's versatility extends far beyond typical use cases. By applying creative thinking and exploring uncharted territory, you can unlock new ways to innovate, grow, and thrive. This section introduces unconventional yet powerful tips to harness ChatGPT, helping you identify untapped markets, craft compelling media kits, and create industry-specific personas.

## 6.11 Using AI to Identify Untapped Markets or Trending Business Ideas

One of ChatGPT's hidden strengths is its ability to generate ideas and insights from patterns and emerging trends. By asking the right questions, you can use AI to uncover profitable niches and business opportunities.

### 6.11.1 Spotting Untapped Markets

ChatGPT can help brainstorm ideas for products, services, or businesses that cater to underserved audiences.

• *Prompt*: "Suggest 5 business ideas for serving eco-conscious millennials in urban areas."

• *Example Output*:

1 Reusable packaging subscription for takeout food.

2 A platform for renting secondhand formal wear.

### 6.11.2 Trend Analysis

ChatGPT can analyze trends and recommend innovative applications for them:

• *Prompt*: "What are emerging trends in the wellness industry, and how can small businesses capitalize on them?"

• *Example Output*:

o Trend: Personalized wellness plans.

○ Application: Offer subscription-based custom fitness plans using AI.

### 6.11.3 Idea Validation

Validate business ideas by testing their viability:

• *Prompt*: "Analyze the potential success of a meal subscription service focused on locally sourced ingredients."

• *Example Output*:

○ Strengths: Growing demand for sustainable food.

○ Challenges: Higher price point due to local sourcing.

**Actionable Tip**: Combine insights from ChatGPT with market research tools like Google Trends or SEMrush for a comprehensive strategy.

## 6.12 Generating Press Releases and Media Kits for Startups

Press releases and media kits are essential for startups looking to make a splash, and ChatGPT can create professional, engaging materials quickly and efficiently.

### 6.12.1 Writing Press Releases

**1 Product Launch**:

○ *Prompt*: "Write a press release for a tech startup launching an app that helps users track their carbon footprint."

○ Example Output:

■ Headline: "CarbonCalc: Revolutionizing Sustainability with AI-Powered Carbon Tracking."

■ Body: "CarbonCalc empowers users to monitor and reduce their carbon footprint with real-time analytics and actionable insights."

**2 Partnership Announcements**:

○ *Prompt*: "Write a press release announcing a partnership

between a local coffee shop and a non-profit supporting sustainable farming."

**3 Milestone Achievements**:
   o *Prompt*: "Draft a press release for a SaaS company celebrating 1 million active users."

### 6.12.2 Crafting Media Kits

A media kit is a crucial resource for startups to attract attention from journalists and partners.

**1 Company Overview**:
   o *Prompt*: "Write a one-paragraph summary of a startup that creates eco-friendly packaging solutions for e-commerce companies."

**2 Founder Bios**:
   o *Prompt*: "Create a professional bio for the founder of a digital marketing agency specializing in AI solutions."

**3 Brand Story**:
   o *Prompt*: "Tell the story of a startup that began as a side hustle and now serves thousands of customers."

**4 FAQs for Media**:
   o *Prompt*: "Write 5 FAQ questions and answers for a press kit about a health tech startup."

**Pro Tip**: Pair ChatGPT-generated content with visually appealing templates using tools like Canva or Adobe InDesign.

## 6.13 Creating Custom ChatGPT Personas for Specific Industries

Customizing ChatGPT to act as a persona tailored for a specific industry or audience can dramatically improve the relevance and impact of its outputs.

### 6.13.1 What are ChatGPT Personas?

A persona is a specialized role that you define for ChatGPT. By instructing the AI to adopt a specific identity, you can tailor its tone, expertise, and style to suit your needs.

## 6.13.2 Examples of Custom Personas
### 1 Virtual Tutor:
○ *Prompt*: "Act as a math tutor for high school students. Explain the Pythagorean theorem with a real-world example."
○ Use Case: Educational businesses or individual learning plans.
### 2 Health Coach:
○ *Prompt*: "You are a health coach. Create a week-long meal plan for someone looking to lose weight and improve energy levels."
○ Use Case: Fitness trainers or wellness apps.
### 3 Legal Assistant:
○ *Prompt*: "You are a legal assistant. Draft a simple contract for a freelance photographer working with a corporate client."
○ Use Case: Law firms or independent consultants.
### 4 Marketing Strategist:
○ *Prompt*: "Act as a marketing strategist for a sustainable fashion brand. Suggest 5 campaigns for promoting a new collection."
○ Use Case: Small businesses or marketing agencies.
### 5 Customer Support Agent:
○ *Prompt*: "You are a customer support agent for an online bookstore. Respond to a query about late delivery in a professional and empathetic tone."
○ Use Case: E-commerce platforms or service providers.

## 6.13.3 How to Build Effective Personas
### 1 Define the Role:
○ Be specific about the industry and tasks.
○ *Prompt*: "You are a financial advisor specializing in retirement planning for small business owners."
### 2 Set the Tone and Style:

○ Specify whether the persona should be formal, casual, or empathetic.

○ *Prompt*: "You are a friendly and approachable personal trainer guiding a beginner."

**3 Add Constraints**:

○ Limit responses to match audience preferences.

○ *Prompt*: "Keep your answers concise and easy for beginners to understand."

**Actionable Tip**: Save commonly used prompts for personas to streamline your workflow.


By exploring these unexpected uses, you can push ChatGPT far beyond traditional applications and unlock innovative opportunities. Whether you're identifying new markets, crafting press releases, or creating specialized personas, these tips help you differentiate yourself in competitive industries and maximize the value ChatGPT brings to your endeavors. The key is to experiment, iterate, and think creatively—because with ChatGPT, the possibilities are truly limitless.

## Chapter 7
# Case Studies and Success Stories

Real-world examples showcase how people and businesses have used ChatGPT to innovate, solve problems, and create revenue streams. This chapter dives into inspiring case studies and success stories from various industries, offering detailed breakdowns, actionable takeaways, and lessons to help you replicate their achievements or adapt them to your needs.

## 7.1 The Freelancer Who Doubled Their Income

**Case Study**: A content writer leveraged ChatGPT to increase productivity, diversify offerings, and scale their business.

### 7.1.1 The Problem

A freelance writer struggled to meet the growing demand for high-quality content while juggling multiple client deadlines. Their challenges included:

- Limited bandwidth to take on new clients.
- Difficulty brainstorming fresh ideas for diverse niches.
- Slow turnaround times affecting client satisfaction.

### 7.1.2 The Solution

The freelancer began using ChatGPT to streamline content creation:

**1 Content Drafting:**

○ *Prompt*: "Write a 1,000-word blog post about the benefits of sustainable fashion for millennials."

○ ChatGPT provided a solid draft that the freelancer edited and personalized.

**2 Idea Generation:**

○ *Prompt*: "Suggest 10 blog post ideas for a travel website focused on adventure tourism."

**3 Client Outreach:**

○ *Prompt*: "Write a professional email pitching my writing services to e-commerce businesses."

### 7.1.3 Results

- **Efficiency Boost**: Reduced average turnaround time for blog posts by 50%.
- **Income Growth**: With the time saved, the freelancer took on 40% more clients, doubling their income.
- **New Offerings**: Added social media content and ad copywriting to their portfolio, attracting a broader client base.

### 7.1.4 Key Takeaways

- Use ChatGPT for time-consuming tasks like drafting and idea generation.
- Personalize AI-generated content to maintain quality and originality.
- Offer diverse services to expand your client base.

## 7.2 The E-Commerce Store That Increased Sales by 30%

**Case Study**: A small e-commerce business used ChatGPT to enhance product descriptions, customer engagement, and marketing strategies.

### 7.2.1 The Problem

The store struggled with:
- Low conversion rates due to unengaging product descriptions.
- High cart abandonment rates.
- Ineffective marketing emails that failed to drive traffic.

### 7.2.2 The Solution

**1 Improved Product Descriptions**:
- *Prompt*: "Write an engaging product description for a luxury leather handbag. Highlight craftsmanship and durability."

**2 Cart Abandonment Emails**:
- *Prompt*: "Create a follow-up email for customers who abandoned their carts. Include a discount code and a sense of urgency."

**3 Marketing Campaigns**:
- *Prompt*: "Draft 5 Facebook ad variations for promoting a winter sale on outdoor gear."

### 7.2.3 Results

- **Increased Conversions**: Enhanced product descriptions led to a 20% increase in purchase rates.
- **Reduced Cart Abandonment**: Follow-up emails recovered 15% of abandoned carts.
- **Boosted Revenue**: Combined efforts resulted in a 30% sales increase within three months.

### 7.2.4 Key Takeaways

- Tailor ChatGPT outputs to fit your brand's voice and target audience.
- Use ChatGPT to create persuasive, customer-focused marketing materials.
- Automate follow-up processes to re-engage potential customers.

## 7.3 The Teacher Who Revolutionized Lesson Planning

**Case Study**: A high school teacher integrated ChatGPT into their workflow to create engaging lessons and personalized materials.

### 7.3.1 The Problem

The teacher faced:

• Limited time to prepare differentiated lessons for students with varying learning needs.

• Difficulty designing creative activities to keep students engaged.

### 7.3.2 The Solution

**1 Lesson Planning**:

○ *Prompt*: "Create a week-long lesson plan for teaching the basics of photosynthesis to 9th graders."

**2 Interactive Activities**:

○ *Prompt*: "Design a classroom activity where students act out the process of photosynthesis."

**3 Quizzes and Worksheets**:

○ *Prompt*: "Generate a 10-question quiz on photosynthesis for high school students."

### 7.3.3 Results

• **Saved Time**: Reduced lesson preparation time by 60%.

• **Enhanced Engagement**: Creative activities led to increased student participation.

• **Improved Learning Outcomes**: Custom quizzes helped identify and address learning gaps.

### 7.3.4 Key Takeaways

• Use ChatGPT to quickly create lesson plans and assessments.

• Incorporate AI-generated activities to make lessons more interactive.

• Adapt ChatGPT outputs to meet individual student needs.

## 7.4 The Startup That Streamlined Customer Support

**Case Study**: A tech startup used ChatGPT to automate and enhance their customer support operations.

### 7.4.1 The Problem

The startup's small team struggled to handle customer queries efficiently, leading to delayed responses and decreased customer satisfaction.

### 7.4.2 The Solution

**1 Automated Chatbot**:
- *Prompt*: "Write chatbot responses for common customer queries about software installation and troubleshooting."

**2 Email Templates**:
- *Prompt*: "Draft a professional response to a customer requesting a refund for a delayed product."

**3 Knowledge Base Articles**:
- *Prompt*: "Create a step-by-step guide for resolving common login issues."

### 7.4.3 Results

- **Faster Response Times**: Reduced average query resolution time by 70%.
- **Cost Savings**: Freed up staff to focus on high-priority tasks by automating routine queries.
- **Improved Customer Satisfaction**: Customer support ratings increased by 25%.

### 7.4.4 Key Takeaways

- Use ChatGPT to create chatbot scripts and email templates for common customer interactions.
- Leverage AI for building a comprehensive knowledge base.
- Focus human resources on complex queries requiring personalized attention.

## 7.5 The Entrepreneur Who Launched a Successful Online Course

**Case Study**: A solopreneur used ChatGPT to create and market an online course on productivity.

### 7.5.1 The Problem

The entrepreneur wanted to monetize their expertise but lacked time to create comprehensive course materials.

### 7.5.2 The Solution

**1 Course Outline**:

○ *Prompt*: "Create a 10-module course outline for teaching productivity skills to remote workers."
  
  **2 Lesson Content**:
  ○ *Prompt*: "Write a script for a video lesson on how to manage distractions while working from home."
  
  **3 Marketing Materials**:
  ○ *Prompt*: "Draft a promotional email campaign for my online course on productivity."

### 7.5.3 Results
- **Faster Launch**: Created a full course in half the time compared to traditional methods.
- **Effective Marketing**: High-converting emails resulted in a 40% increase in sign-ups.
- **Revenue Growth**: Generated $10,000 in sales within the first month of launch.

### 7.5.4 Key Takeaways
- Use ChatGPT to generate course outlines, lesson scripts, and promotional content.
- Pair AI-generated materials with personal expertise for authenticity.
- Leverage email marketing to maximize course enrollment.

## 7.6 Key Lessons from Success Stories
**1 Combine AI with Human Expertise**:
  ○ ChatGPT excels at generating drafts, but your unique input and insights add value and originality.

**2 Scale and Diversify Offerings**:
  ○ Use ChatGPT to explore new services or products that were previously too time-intensive.

**3 Experiment and Iterate**:
  ○ Success often comes from refining ChatGPT outputs through testing and feedback.

. . .

## 7.7 Actionable Steps to Apply These Strategies

• **Identify Your Pain Points**: List tasks or challenges in your workflow that ChatGPT can assist with.

• **Start Small**: Test ChatGPT with a single project (e.g., drafting emails or creating lesson plans) before scaling up.

• **Personalize Outputs**: Edit and adapt AI-generated content to ensure it aligns with your voice and goals.

• **Track Results**: Measure the impact of ChatGPT on your efficiency, revenue, or customer satisfaction.


These case studies demonstrate that ChatGPT isn't just a tool—it's a transformative ally for achieving success across industries. Whether you're a freelancer, entrepreneur, teacher, or business owner, these real-world examples provide inspiration and actionable guidance for leveraging ChatGPT in your own journey. The next chapter will explore ethical considerations and challenges in AI use, equipping you to navigate the evolving landscape responsibly and effectively.

# Chapter 8
# Ethical Considerations and AI Challenges

As powerful and transformative as ChatGPT and generative AI can be, they also come with ethical considerations and challenges that must be navigated carefully. This chapter explores these issues, offering in-depth explanations, real-world examples, and actionable guidance for using AI responsibly. Understanding and addressing these concerns will not only protect your reputation but also help you create trust with your audience, clients, or customers.

## 8.1 Navigating Ethical Dilemmas in AI-Generated Work

Generative AI has raised several ethical questions, from intellectual property concerns to the potential for misuse. Navigating these dilemmas is essential for maintaining credibility and integrity.

### 8.1.1 Ownership and Attribution

**Challenge**: Who owns the content generated by AI? And should you disclose AI's involvement?

**Guidance**:

**1 Understand Platform Policies**:

o Platforms like OpenAI clarify that users own the outputs generated by ChatGPT, but it's essential to verify specific terms of use.

o *Example*: A freelance writer using ChatGPT for client work must ensure that their outputs comply with copyright laws.

**2 Disclose When Necessary**:

o Transparency builds trust. If your audience or clients value originality, disclose that AI was used as a tool.

o *Best Practice*: Include a note such as, "This content was created with the assistance of AI and refined by [your name]."

### 8.1.2 Authenticity and Plagiarism

**Challenge**: AI may generate content that resembles existing material, raising concerns about plagiarism or lack of originality.

**Guidance**:

**1 Run Outputs Through Plagiarism Checkers**:

o Tools like Copyscape or Grammarly's plagiarism checker can help ensure originality.

o *Example*: Before submitting a blog post, verify that the content isn't inadvertently copied from another source.

**2 Refine and Personalize Outputs**:

o Always edit and add your unique voice or insights to AI-generated content.

o *Example*: A marketing professional using ChatGPT to draft ad copy should add brand-specific language and creative elements.

### 8.1.3 Bias in AI Outputs

**Challenge**: AI models are trained on large datasets that may contain biases, leading to problematic or discriminatory outputs.

**Guidance**:

**1 Audit AI Outputs**:

○ Review all outputs critically to identify and remove any potential bias.

○ *Example*: A recruiter using ChatGPT to write job descriptions should ensure inclusive language that doesn't inadvertently discourage certain groups from applying.

**2 Provide Context in Prompts**:

○ Be specific about avoiding bias when crafting prompts.

○ *Prompt*: "Write an unbiased and inclusive job description for a software developer role."

## 8.2 Addressing Plagiarism, Intellectual Property, and Authenticity

Intellectual property and originality are critical concerns when using AI-generated work. Missteps in these areas can lead to legal issues or loss of trust.

### 8.2.1 Safeguarding Intellectual Property

**Challenge**: AI-generated content might inadvertently mimic existing copyrighted material.

**Guidance**:

**1 Understand Copyright Law**:

○ AI-generated content is considered derivative unless explicitly verified as unique.

○ *Example*: A graphic designer using AI-generated images must ensure the final product doesn't infringe on existing copyrighted works.

**2 Use Outputs as Starting Points**:

○ Treat AI outputs as drafts to build upon rather than final products.

○ *Example*: Use ChatGPT's product descriptions as a base, then rewrite them to make them fully original.

### 8.2.2 Establishing Authenticity

**Challenge**: Over-reliance on AI can lead to content that feels generic or lacks a personal touch.

**Guidance**:

**1 Integrate Personal Stories or Insights**:
- Add examples, anecdotes, or expertise that only you can provide.
- *Example*: A consultant writing an article on leadership should include lessons learned from their own experiences.

**2 Maintain Your Brand Voice**:
- Ensure AI-generated content matches your unique tone and style.
- *Prompt*: "Write this article in a professional but conversational tone suitable for a leadership blog."

## 8.3 Managing Client and Audience Expectations

Transparency and trust are essential when using AI for professional purposes. Managing expectations about AI's role can prevent misunderstandings.

### 8.3.1 Setting Clear Boundaries

**1 Define AI's Role**:
- Clearly explain how AI is being used in your workflow.
- *Example*: A freelance writer might tell clients, "AI helps me brainstorm ideas and structure drafts, but I personally review and edit all content."

**2 Avoid Overpromising**:
- AI is a tool, not a magic solution. Be realistic about its capabilities.
- *Example*: When building chatbots, set clear expectations about their limitations, such as being unable to handle highly complex queries.

. . .

### 8.3.2 Educating Clients and Stakeholders

**1 Demonstrate Value:**

- Show how AI improves efficiency without sacrificing quality.
- *Example*: A marketer might explain that AI speeds up the process of generating ad copy, allowing more time for creative strategy.

**2 Highlight Human Oversight:**

- Emphasize that final outputs are reviewed or refined by a professional.
- *Example*: A law firm using AI for drafting contracts should clarify that attorneys verify all outputs for legal accuracy.

## 8.4 Preparing for Ethical Challenges in Emerging AI Applications

As AI continues to evolve, new ethical challenges are likely to arise. Staying informed and proactive is key to navigating these issues.

### 8.4.1 Ethical Use of AI in Automation

**1 Avoid Job Displacement Concerns:**

- Use AI to complement human workers, not replace them.
- *Example*: An HR team automating resume screening should use AI as a first pass, with human recruiters making final decisions.

**2 Balance Efficiency with Empathy:**

- Ensure customer-facing AI tools, like chatbots, provide a human-like touch.
- *Prompt*: "Write chatbot responses that are empathetic and professional for a mental health support platform."

### 8.4.2 Mitigating Risks of Deepfake and Misinformation

**1 Verify Sources:**

- Cross-check AI-generated information against trusted resources.

o *Example*: When creating educational content, ensure accuracy by consulting reputable references.

**2 Avoid Misleading Outputs**:

o Never use AI to generate content that could intentionally mislead or harm.

o *Example*: Avoid creating fake reviews or testimonials for products.

## 8.5 Actionable Tips for Responsible AI Use

### 8.5.1 Develop a Code of Ethics

Create clear guidelines for how you or your organization will use AI. This might include:
- Transparency with clients and users.
- Regular reviews of AI outputs for bias or errors.
- Commitment to refining outputs for quality and originality.

### 8.5.2 Invest in Continuous Learning

**1 Stay Informed**:

o Follow updates in AI ethics and legislation to adapt your practices.

o *Example*: Learn about GDPR compliance if using AI for data-driven tasks in Europe.

**2 Experiment Responsibly**:

o Test AI outputs in low-risk scenarios before deploying them publicly.

o *Example*: Use AI for internal brainstorming before rolling out a full campaign.

### 8.5.3 Build Accountability Mechanisms

**1 Establish Review Processes**:

o Ensure all AI-generated content is checked by a human editor.

o *Example*: Use ChatGPT to generate initial drafts, but implement a mandatory review step before publishing.
   **2 Solicit Feedback**:
    o Regularly gather input from clients or users to improve AI applications.
    o *Example*: If deploying an AI-powered chatbot, monitor customer satisfaction and adjust as needed.

## 8.6 Real-World Examples of Ethical Challenges and Solutions

### Example 1: AI in Hiring

**Challenge**: A company's AI tool unintentionally excluded female candidates by favoring historically male-dominated job descriptions. **Solution**: Updated the tool to prioritize neutral language and introduced human oversight.

### Example 2: Chatbot Miscommunication

**Challenge**: An AI-powered customer service chatbot gave incorrect advice about refunds, frustrating users. **Solution**: Added specific parameters to ChatGPT's training data and implemented manual escalation for complex queries.

Ethical considerations and challenges are an inevitable part of using advanced AI like ChatGPT. By prioritizing transparency, accuracy, and accountability, you can use AI responsibly while maintaining trust with your audience, clients, or stakeholders. Addressing these issues proactively ensures that you not only maximize AI's benefits but also contribute to its positive integration into society. In the next chapter, we'll explore future trends and opportunities in generative AI, equipping you to stay ahead of the curve in an ever-evolving field.

# Chapter 9
# Future Trends and Opportunities in AI

Artificial intelligence, and particularly generative AI like ChatGPT, is rapidly reshaping industries, creating new opportunities, and transforming how we work and live. This chapter explores the emerging trends and potential applications of AI across different sectors, offering actionable insights and guidance to help you stay ahead in an ever-evolving landscape. Whether you're an entrepreneur, developer, or educator, understanding these trends will enable you to harness AI's potential for innovation and growth.

## 9.1 The Evolving Landscape of Generative AI Tools

Generative AI is at the forefront of technological advancements, and its capabilities are constantly expanding. These advancements open doors to new applications, business models, and industries.

### 9.1.1 Key Trends in Generative AI
**1 Multimodal AI**:
- Generative AI tools are evolving from text-only capabilities to

multimodal functionalities, allowing them to process and generate text, images, audio, and video.

o *Example*: OpenAI's DALL·E can generate images from text descriptions, while tools like ElevenLabs can produce human-like voiceovers.

**2 Context-Aware AI**:

o Models are becoming more adept at understanding context, enabling more nuanced and accurate outputs.

o *Example*: ChatGPT's API can be trained to understand customer-specific contexts for personalized customer service.

**3 AI-Driven Collaboration**:

o AI tools are increasingly being integrated into collaborative environments, enhancing teamwork.

o *Example*: Microsoft Copilot integrates generative AI into Office apps, enabling users to brainstorm ideas or summarize documents directly in Word or Excel.

## 9.1.2 The Rise of AI Specialization

Generic AI tools are giving way to specialized models tailored to specific industries and tasks:

• *Healthcare*: AI models trained on medical datasets to assist with diagnostics and treatment plans.

• *Education*: AI tutors personalized for different learning styles and subject areas.

• *Legal*: Tools that generate contracts, analyze legal documents, or assist with case law research.

**Actionable Guidance**:

• Explore specialized AI tools within your field to gain a competitive edge.

• *Example*: Use an AI-powered platform like PathAI for medical diagnostics or Jasper for tailored marketing content.

## 9.2 Emerging Applications in Key Industries

AI is transforming industries at an unprecedented rate. Here's a closer look at how generative AI is making its mark.

### 9.2.1 Education

**1 Personalized Learning**:
- AI-driven tutors create custom lesson plans and adaptive quizzes based on individual learning needs.
- *Example*: An AI tutor provides real-time feedback and custom exercises for students struggling with algebra.

**2 Content Creation for Educators**:
- Teachers can use ChatGPT to generate lesson plans, quizzes, and interactive activities.
- *Prompt*: "Design a week-long lesson plan for teaching the basics of coding to middle school students."

**3 Language Learning**:
- Generative AI provides immersive language practice by simulating conversations.
- *Example*: A virtual Spanish tutor roleplays real-world scenarios like ordering food or asking for directions.

### 9.2.2 Healthcare

**1 Patient Education**:
- AI can simplify complex medical terms and explain diagnoses in layman's terms.
- *Prompt*: "Write a patient-friendly explanation of hypertension and how to manage it."

**2 Mental Health Support**:
- Chatbots provide empathetic, conversational support for users struggling with stress or anxiety.
- *Example*: AI tools like Woebot use generative AI to deliver cognitive behavioral therapy techniques.

**3 Clinical Research**:

- AI accelerates drug discovery by analyzing data and suggesting potential compounds.
- *Example*: Generative AI models assist pharmaceutical companies in designing novel drugs.

### 9.2.3 Business and E-Commerce
**1 Product Development**:
- AI generates ideas for new products based on market trends.
- *Prompt*: "Suggest innovative product ideas for a sustainable fashion brand."

**2 Customer Support**:
- AI chatbots provide instant support, answering queries or resolving issues 24/7.
- *Example*: E-commerce companies use ChatGPT-powered chatbots to reduce response times.

**3 Business Analytics**:
- Generative AI simplifies data analysis by providing actionable insights from complex datasets.
- *Prompt*: "Summarize this sales data and suggest strategies for improving Q4 performance."

### 9.2.4 Creative Industries
**1 Content Generation**:
- AI assists in writing scripts, generating art, or composing music.
- *Example*: Writers use ChatGPT to brainstorm story ideas or draft dialogues.

**2 Game Design**:
- Generative AI creates immersive worlds, characters, and narratives for video games.
- *Prompt*: "Design a fantasy RPG storyline involving a hero, a lost kingdom, and a magical artifact."

**3 Marketing Campaigns**:

o AI generates ad copy, social media posts, and campaign ideas tailored to specific audiences.

o *Example*: Jasper and Copy.ai offer AI-driven content for digital marketing.

## 9.3 Preparing for a World Integrated with AI

As AI becomes more pervasive, adapting to this new reality is essential for professionals and businesses alike.

### 9.3.1 Reskilling and Upskilling
**1 AI Literacy**:

o Understand the basics of how generative AI works and its capabilities.

o *Example*: Take online courses like Coursera's "AI for Everyone" to build foundational knowledge.

**2 Prompt Engineering**:

o Learn how to craft effective prompts to maximize AI outputs.

o *Prompt*: "Explain how prompt specificity impacts the quality of ChatGPT responses."

**3 Collaboration Skills**:

o Develop strategies for integrating AI tools into existing workflows.

o *Example*: A project manager might use AI to automate routine updates while focusing on strategic tasks.

### 9.3.2 Ethical and Social Considerations
**1 AI in the Workforce**:

o Balance AI adoption with maintaining and creating jobs.

o *Example*: Use AI for repetitive tasks while investing in employee training for creative or strategic roles.

**2 AI Bias and Fairness**:

o Ensure AI systems are audited for bias and inclusivity.

- *Example*: A hiring manager using AI for resume screening should verify that the tool avoids discriminatory practices.

**3 Transparency and Trust**:
- Clearly communicate when and how AI is being used in customer-facing interactions.
- *Prompt*: "Generate a statement explaining how our company uses AI to enhance customer experiences."

## 9.4 Emerging Business Models and Opportunities

AI is enabling entirely new business models and opportunities.

### 9.4.1 Subscription-Based AI Tools

**1 Content as a Service**:
- Businesses offer AI-generated content on a subscription basis.
- *Example*: A company provides weekly SEO-optimized blog posts for small businesses using ChatGPT.

**2 AI Coaching Platforms**:
- Personalized AI coaching for fitness, mental health, or career development.
- *Example*: An AI coach creates daily fitness plans tailored to individual goals and preferences.

### 9.4.2 AI-Driven Marketplaces

Platforms are emerging to connect users with AI services:

**1 AI App Stores**:
- Curated libraries of AI tools tailored for specific industries.
- *Example*: Microsoft and Google provide AI-driven plugins for business applications.

**2 Custom AI Services**:
- Freelancers and businesses offer bespoke AI solutions, such as automated workflows or tailored chatbots.
- *Example*: A startup creates AI chatbots for non-profits to streamline donor communication.

## 9.5 Actionable Steps to Stay Ahead in AI

**1 Experiment with AI Tools:**
- Regularly test new AI platforms and tools to stay informed about their capabilities.
- *Example*: Try tools like MidJourney for design or Jasper for marketing content.

**2 Build a Personal AI Toolkit:**
- Identify and adopt tools that align with your goals.
- *Example*: Use ChatGPT for writing, Grammarly for editing, and DALL·E for visual design.

**3 Collaborate and Innovate:**
- Partner with developers or AI-focused businesses to create unique solutions.
- *Example*: A marketer partners with an AI developer to create a custom content-generation tool.

The future of AI is brimming with possibilities. By staying informed about trends, embracing emerging applications, and investing in skills to collaborate effectively with AI, you can position yourself at the forefront of innovation. As generative AI continues to evolve, those who adapt and harness its capabilities responsibly will unlock unparalleled opportunities for success. The next chapter will guide you through resources, tools, and communities that can help you continue your AI journey.

## Chapter 10
# Resources and Tools for Amplifying ChatGPT's Functionality

ChatGPT is a powerful tool on its own, but its potential expands exponentially when combined with the right resources, tools, and platforms. This chapter provides a comprehensive guide to the best tools, communities, and strategies for leveraging ChatGPT to its fullest. Whether you're a beginner or an experienced AI user, these resources will help you amplify ChatGPT's capabilities, streamline your workflow, and open up new opportunities.

## 10.1 Must-Have AI Tools to Amplify ChatGPT's Functionality

Integrating ChatGPT with other AI tools can enhance its power and versatility, making it a central part of your workflow. Below are tools that complement ChatGPT across different use cases.

### 10.1.1 Tools for Content Creation
**1 Grammarly**:
- Enhances grammar, spelling, and clarity for AI-generated content.

○ *Example*: After using ChatGPT to draft an article, Grammarly ensures the final piece is polished and professional.

**2 Canva**:

○ Ideal for pairing ChatGPT's text outputs with visual elements for presentations, social media, and marketing materials.

○ *Example*: Generate a social media caption using ChatGPT, then design an engaging post in Canva.

**3 SurferSEO**:

○ Combines AI-generated content with SEO optimization tools.

○ *Example*: Use ChatGPT to draft a blog post, and SurferSEO to optimize it for search engines with relevant keywords and structure.

## 10.1.2 Tools for Developers

**1 GitHub Copilot**:

○ A code-completion tool that works alongside ChatGPT for coding projects.

○ *Example*: Use ChatGPT to draft algorithms, and GitHub Copilot to refine and debug your code.

**2 Postman**:

○ A tool for API testing and development, ideal for integrating ChatGPT's API into larger systems.

○ *Example*: Test ChatGPT-generated APIs for chatbot deployment using Postman.

**3 Zapier**:

○ Automates workflows by connecting ChatGPT with other apps and tools.

○ *Example*: Automate the process of generating and publishing blog posts by linking ChatGPT, Google Docs, and WordPress.

## 10.1.3 Tools for Business Applications

**1 HubSpot**:

- A CRM tool that works well with AI-generated email campaigns and customer responses.
- *Example*: Use ChatGPT to create personalized email templates, then schedule and send them via HubSpot.

**2 Notion**:
- A project management tool that integrates with ChatGPT for task automation.
- *Example*: Use ChatGPT to generate meeting notes or task lists, then organize them in Notion.

**3 Hootsuite**:
- Manages social media scheduling and monitoring, complementing ChatGPT-generated captions and posts.
- *Example*: Draft a month's worth of Instagram posts with ChatGPT and schedule them on Hootsuite.

## 10.2 Recommended Platforms for Freelancing and Selling Content

Freelancers and entrepreneurs can monetize ChatGPT by using platforms designed for selling content, offering services, or building businesses.

### 10.2.1 Platforms for Freelancers

**1 Upwork**:
- A freelancing platform where you can offer AI-enhanced services like content creation, chatbot design, or marketing.
- *Example*: Advertise your ability to create SEO-optimized blog posts using ChatGPT.

**2 Fiverr**:
- Focuses on quick gigs, making it ideal for selling niche AI-driven services.
- *Example*: Offer personalized greeting card messages, resume writing, or product descriptions powered by ChatGPT.

**3 Toptal**:

o A platform for high-level freelancers, ideal for developers integrating ChatGPT APIs into custom applications.

### 10.2.2 Platforms for Selling Content
**1 Etsy**:
o Perfect for selling creative outputs like personalized poems, greeting cards, or e-books.

o *Example*: Use ChatGPT to generate wedding vows or anniversary messages and sell them as digital downloads.

**2 Amazon Kindle Direct Publishing (KDP)**:
o A self-publishing platform for e-books and print-on-demand paperbacks.

o *Example*: Write a children's book or a niche guidebook with ChatGPT and publish it on KDP.

**3 Gumroad**:
o A platform for selling digital products directly to your audience.

o *Example*: Offer AI-generated online courses, templates, or newsletters.

## 10.3 Communities, Blogs, and Forums for Continued Learning

Staying updated on AI trends and exchanging ideas with others can help you improve your skills and discover new applications.

### 10.3.1 Online Communities
**1 Reddit**:
o Subreddits like r/ChatGPT or r/OpenAI provide discussions, tips, and use-case ideas.

o *Example*: Share your ChatGPT successes and learn advanced prompt techniques from others.

**2 Discord Servers**:

- Join AI-focused Discord communities to network with like-minded individuals and collaborate on projects.

**3 LinkedIn Groups**:
- Engage with professionals using AI in business or education.
- *Example*: Follow LinkedIn groups like "AI for Business" for industry-specific insights.

### 10.3.2 AI-Focused Blogs

**1 Towards Data Science**:
- A blog with tutorials and thought leadership on AI trends and technologies.
- *Example*: Read case studies on integrating ChatGPT into enterprise solutions.

**2 OpenAI Blog**:
- Stay updated on the latest advancements and releases from OpenAI.

**3 Medium**:
- Explore user-written articles on generative AI use cases, tutorials, and prompt engineering tips.

### 10.3.3 AI-Focused YouTube Channels

**1 TechLead**:
- Provides tutorials and insights into leveraging AI for development and entrepreneurship.

**2 ColdFusion**:
- Explores how AI is transforming industries and global economies.

**3 AI Explained**:
- Covers updates, tools, and creative uses of AI.

## 10.4 Actionable Steps to Build Your AI Toolkit

**1 Assess Your Needs:**

○ Identify your primary goals (e.g., content creation, automation, coding).

○ *Example*: A marketer might prioritize tools for social media and SEO, while a developer focuses on APIs.

**2 Experiment with Tools:**

○ Try different platforms to find what works best for your workflow.

○ *Example*: Test Grammarly and Hemingway to refine AI-generated articles.

**3 Invest in Premium Features:**

○ Upgrading to pro versions of tools can unlock additional functionality.

○ *Example*: DALL·E Pro offers higher-quality image generation for creative projects.

## 10.5 Combining Resources for Maximum Impact

**1 Workflow Automation:**

○ Use Zapier to automate repetitive tasks, combining ChatGPT with tools like Google Sheets and Slack.

○ *Example*: Automatically generate and distribute meeting summaries after each Zoom call.

**2 Multimodal AI Solutions:**

○ Pair ChatGPT with image-generation tools like MidJourney or DALL·E.

○ *Example*: Create a blog post using ChatGPT and illustrate it with DALL·E-generated images.

**3 Custom Integrations:**

○ Use APIs to build unique applications tailored to your needs.

○ *Example*: Integrate ChatGPT with your CRM system to generate custom email responses.

. . .

## 10.6 Building a Network of AI Professionals

Collaboration with other AI users can enhance your learning and expand your opportunities.

**1 Join Industry Events**:
- Attend conferences like AI Expo or Web Summit to network with professionals using AI in innovative ways.

**2 Collaborate on Projects**:
- Partner with developers, designers, or marketers to create unique AI-powered solutions.

**3 Seek Mentorship**:
- Engage with experienced AI professionals to learn best practices and stay updated on trends.

ChatGPT's capabilities are amplified when paired with the right resources and tools. By leveraging these platforms, communities, and strategies, you can optimize your workflow, scale your business, and stay ahead in an AI-driven world. With a robust toolkit and an ever-growing network of collaborators, the possibilities for innovation and growth are virtually limitless. The next and final chapter will outline your roadmap to sustained success, summarizing the journey and providing actionable next steps for your AI-powered future.

# Chapter 11
# Conclusion and Next Steps for AI-Powered Success

As we reach the end of this journey into the world of ChatGPT and generative AI, this chapter ties everything together. It recaps key insights, provides actionable steps to help you start or refine your AI-powered initiatives, and inspires you to innovate, adapt, and stay ahead in an ever-changing AI landscape. Whether you're a freelancer, entrepreneur, educator, or enthusiast, these next steps will help you turn knowledge into sustained success.

## 11.1 Recap of Key Takeaways

Over the past chapters, we've explored how to harness ChatGPT and generative AI for productivity, creativity, and monetization. Let's revisit the most impactful lessons:

### 11.1.1 Understanding ChatGPT's Capabilities

- **Generative Power**: ChatGPT excels in content creation, problem-solving, and idea generation across various industries.
- **Scalability**: AI enables you to do more in less time, making it a valuable tool for individuals and teams.
- **Customization**: Tailoring prompts and workflows unlocks

ChatGPT's full potential, allowing you to deliver high-quality, personalized outputs.

### 11.1.2 Building Practical Applications

- **Freelancing and Monetization**: Chapter 4 showcased strategies for generating income, from offering writing services to creating digital products.
- **Automation and Efficiency**: Chapter 5 demonstrated how to streamline workflows by integrating ChatGPT with automation tools like Zapier or APIs.
- **Creativity and Innovation**: Chapter 6 revealed unexpected ways to use ChatGPT, such as writing children's books, designing games, and generating quizzes.

### 11.1.3 Ethical and Strategic Use

- **Transparency and Trust**: Chapter 8 emphasized the importance of responsible AI use, including plagiarism checks and ethical considerations.
- **Future-Readiness**: Chapter 9 prepared you to adapt to emerging AI trends, such as multimodal tools and AI-specialized solutions.

## 11.2 Actionable Next Steps

To ensure your success in leveraging ChatGPT and generative AI, follow these concrete steps:

### 11.2.1 Assess Your Current Position

Evaluate your current AI knowledge, tools, and use cases to identify areas for improvement.

- *Example*: If you're a content creator, assess how ChatGPT can save time or improve quality in your writing workflow.
- *Prompt*: "How can I integrate ChatGPT into my workflow to save 5 hours per week?"

### 11.2.2 Build a Tailored AI Strategy

**1 Define Your Goals:**

o Are you aiming to increase productivity, create new revenue streams, or enhance customer experiences?

o *Example*: An educator might focus on using AI for personalized learning materials, while a marketer may aim to scale ad campaigns.

**2 Select Tools and Resources:**

o Choose tools that align with your objectives.

o *Example*: Use ChatGPT for writing and DALL·E for visuals in content marketing projects.

**3 Start Small and Scale Gradually:**

o Begin with a single task or project to build confidence and refine your approach.

o *Example*: Use ChatGPT to draft blog posts before expanding to creating social media campaigns or e-books.

## 11.2.3 Invest in Continuous Learning

The AI landscape evolves rapidly, so staying updated is essential.

**1 Take Courses:**

o Platforms like Coursera, Udemy, and LinkedIn Learning offer courses on AI applications, prompt engineering, and AI ethics.

**2 Join Communities:**

o Engage with forums, LinkedIn groups, or Discord servers dedicated to AI and generative tools.

**3 Experiment Regularly:**

o Use new AI features or platforms to expand your skillset.

o *Example*: Experiment with OpenAI's API to create custom applications tailored to your business.

## 11.2.4 Collaborate and Innovate

AI thrives in collaborative environments, where diverse perspectives unlock creative solutions.

- **Form AI Partnerships**:
  - Partner with developers, designers, or marketers to explore unique use cases.
- **Encourage Team Adoption**:
  - Introduce ChatGPT to your team with clear training and best practices.
  - *Example*: Use ChatGPT to automate meeting summaries, freeing up team members for strategic tasks.

### 11.2.5 Track and Optimize Results

Measure the impact of your AI applications to refine and improve your strategies.

**1 Set KPIs**:
- Define key performance indicators such as time saved, revenue growth, or content quality improvements.
- *Example*: Track how much faster you can produce blog posts with ChatGPT.

**2 Review Regularly**:
- Analyze AI's effectiveness and adjust your workflows accordingly.
- *Example*: If customer feedback on AI-generated support responses is mixed, refine your chatbot prompts for clarity and empathy.

## 11.3 Inspiration to Innovate and Adapt

The journey with AI doesn't end here—it evolves as new opportunities emerge. Here are some inspiring ideas to keep you motivated:

### 11.3.1 Explore Niche Opportunities

Find underserved markets or unique applications for ChatGPT in your industry.

- *Example*: A fitness trainer creates a subscription-based AI coach offering personalized workout plans and meal prep guides.

### 11.3.2 Pioneer New Use Cases

Challenge yourself to innovate in areas where AI hasn't been widely applied.

• *Example*: A nonprofit organization uses ChatGPT to generate grant proposals and outreach materials, amplifying its fundraising efforts.

### 11.3.3 Share Your Knowledge

As you grow, contribute to the AI community by sharing your experiences and successes.

- **Start a Blog or YouTube Channel**:
  - Share tutorials, case studies, or tips on leveraging ChatGPT.
- **Host Workshops**:
  - Teach others how to integrate ChatGPT into their workflows.

## 11.4 Your Roadmap to AI-Powered Success

To simplify your path forward, here's a step-by-step roadmap:

**Step 1: Learn**
- Master ChatGPT's capabilities and potential use cases.
- Explore tutorials, blogs, and communities to refine your skills.

**Step 2: Experiment**
- Test ChatGPT on small projects or tasks, refining your prompts and workflows.

**Step 3: Build**
- Develop AI-powered solutions tailored to your industry or goals.

**Step 4: Scale**
- Expand your AI applications, integrating them into larger workflows or offering them as services.

**Step 5: Innovate**

• Push boundaries by exploring niche opportunities or combining AI tools in unique ways.

**Step 6: Share**

• Contribute to the AI community through tutorials, case studies, or mentorship.

**The Future is AI-Powered—And It's Yours to Shape**

ChatGPT and generative AI offer limitless potential, empowering individuals and businesses to achieve more, innovate faster, and explore new possibilities. By mastering its use and combining it with creativity, collaboration, and ethical practices, you can position yourself as a leader in the AI-powered world.

The journey ahead will require curiosity, adaptability, and continuous learning. But with the tools and strategies outlined in this book, you have everything you need to turn AI into a catalyst for personal and professional success. Now it's time to take the first step—and let ChatGPT help you shape the future.

# Frequently Asked Questions

This FAQ section addresses common questions about the concepts, strategies, and tools discussed in the book. Whether you're a beginner or an experienced AI user, these answers provide clarity, actionable advice, and solutions to potential challenges.

## Getting Started with ChatGPT

**1. What is ChatGPT, and how does it work?**

ChatGPT is a generative AI model developed by OpenAI. It uses natural language processing (NLP) to generate human-like text based on prompts. It works by predicting the next word in a sentence, trained on vast datasets to understand context and generate coherent responses.

**2. Do I need technical knowledge to use ChatGPT effectively?**

No technical knowledge is required to start using ChatGPT. However, learning prompt engineering (crafting effective prompts) and understanding basic AI concepts can greatly enhance your results. Beginners can start with simple queries and progress to more complex applications with practice.

### 3. How do I set up and access ChatGPT?
1 Visit the OpenAI website and create an account.
2 Choose a plan (free or paid, such as ChatGPT Plus).
3 Access ChatGPT via the OpenAI interface or API for advanced integrations.
4 Explore platforms like ChatGPT's web app, desktop apps, or integrated tools (e.g., Microsoft Word with AI).

## Using ChatGPT for Productivity and Creativity

### 4. How can I use ChatGPT to save time in my daily workflow?
ChatGPT can:
- Draft emails and reports.
- Generate content outlines, summaries, and ideas.
- Automate repetitive tasks like customer support queries.
- Suggest improvements to existing work, such as editing or rephrasing.

*Example*: Use ChatGPT to draft meeting agendas and follow-up emails, saving hours weekly.

### 5. Can ChatGPT help with personal projects, like writing books or planning events?
Yes, ChatGPT can:
- Generate book ideas, plots, and character outlines.
- Help draft speeches, poems, or essays.
- Suggest themes, itineraries, or scripts for events.

*Example*: Prompt ChatGPT with "Suggest a detailed itinerary for a three-day family vacation in New York."

# Frequently Asked Questions

## Advanced Applications

### 6. How do I integrate ChatGPT with other tools for automation?

You can use platforms like Zapier or APIs to connect ChatGPT with apps like Google Sheets, Slack, or WordPress. For example:

• Automate blog drafts: Use Zapier to pull blog topics from a spreadsheet, generate drafts via ChatGPT, and upload them to WordPress.

• Customer service workflows: Combine ChatGPT with CRM tools like HubSpot for automated replies and follow-ups.

### 7. Can I use ChatGPT to create an AI-powered business?

Yes, ChatGPT can help launch and scale businesses such as:

• Content creation services (blogs, social media posts, e-books).
• Chatbot development for customer support.
• AI-driven marketing campaigns or SEO services.
• Subscription-based AI tools offering customized outputs.

## Monetization Strategies

### 8. How can I make money using ChatGPT?

The book details several monetization strategies:

**1 Freelance Writing**: Offer blog posts, ad copy, and product descriptions.

**2 Digital Products**: Sell e-books, templates, or online courses created with ChatGPT.

**3 E-Commerce**: Use ChatGPT to enhance product descriptions, ads, and customer interactions.

**4 AI Consulting**: Provide tailored solutions for businesses integrating AI.

## Frequently Asked Questions

### 9. What are some unique, lesser-known ways to monetize ChatGPT?
1 Write children's books with AI-generated stories.
2 Design board games or escape room narratives.
3 Offer personalized greeting card messages for special occasions.
4 Create niche quizzes and trivia for websites or events.
5 Provide grant writing or legal drafting services using AI.

## Prompt Engineering and Optimization

### 10. What are some tips for crafting better prompts?
**1 Be Specific**: Provide detailed context and constraints.
o *Prompt*: "Write a 500-word blog post on the benefits of remote work for small businesses."
**2 Set the Role**: Ask ChatGPT to act in a specific role.
o *Prompt*: "Act as a marketing strategist. Suggest a campaign for launching a fitness app."
**3 Iterate and Refine**: Use follow-up prompts to improve responses.
o *Prompt*: "Rewrite this email with a more professional tone."

### 11. Can I use pre-built prompts to save time?
Yes! Use prompt libraries or templates for recurring tasks, such as:
- Generating SEO-optimized blog outlines.
- Writing cold emails for sales.
- Creating customer service scripts.

## Ethical Considerations

### 12. Is it ethical to use ChatGPT for professional work?
Yes, as long as:
- You disclose AI's role in content creation when relevant (e.g., client work).

## Frequently Asked Questions

• You refine AI-generated outputs to ensure originality and quality.

• You avoid using ChatGPT to plagiarize or create harmful content.

### 13. How do I ensure AI outputs are accurate and unbiased?

1 Cross-check factual information with reliable sources.

2 Rephrase prompts to encourage neutrality and inclusivity.

o *Prompt*: "Write a non-biased job description for a software engineer."

## Challenges and Troubleshooting

### 14. What if ChatGPT doesn't generate the response I need?

1 Rephrase your prompt to provide more context.

o *Prompt*: "List 10 eco-friendly business ideas targeting millennials in urban areas."

2 Break complex tasks into smaller steps.

o Start with "Generate 3 business ideas," then refine each one.

### 15. How do I avoid repetitive or generic responses?

1 Use constraints in your prompts.

o *Prompt*: "Suggest 5 unique campaign ideas for a luxury car brand targeting Gen Z."

2 Request creativity.

o *Prompt*: "Write a humorous social media caption for a pizza delivery service."

## Integrating ChatGPT into Industries

### 16. How can businesses use ChatGPT to improve operations?

## Frequently Asked Questions

**1 Customer Service**: Automate responses to FAQs or design chatbots for 24/7 support.

**2 Marketing**: Generate ad copy, email campaigns, and product descriptions.

**3 Data Analysis**: Use ChatGPT to summarize reports and suggest actionable insights.

### 17. How can educators use ChatGPT?

1 Create lesson plans and quizzes.

   o *Prompt*: "Generate a week-long lesson plan on the basics of climate change for 10th graders."

2 Simplify complex topics.

   o *Prompt*: "Explain the theory of relativity in simple terms for high school students."

## Future Trends

### 18. What's next for generative AI?

**1 Multimodal AI**: Tools that handle text, images, and audio seamlessly.

**2 Industry-Specific AI**: Models fine-tuned for healthcare, legal, or educational applications.

**3 AI Augmentation**: Integrations with AR/VR and IoT devices.

### 19. How can I stay updated on AI developments?

1 Follow AI-focused blogs like *Towards Data Science* or OpenAI's official blog.

2 Join communities like r/ChatGPT or LinkedIn groups.

3 Attend AI conferences and webinars.

## Getting the Most Out of This Book

### 20. How do I apply what I've learned in this book?

## Frequently Asked Questions

**1 Start Small**: Experiment with one task or project to build confidence.
- *Example*: Use ChatGPT for drafting blog posts before expanding to broader business applications.

**2 Iterate and Refine**: Adjust your approach based on results and feedback.

**3 Explore Monetization**: Identify opportunities in your field to turn AI-powered outputs into income streams.

## 21. What's the most important thing to remember about using ChatGPT?

ChatGPT is a tool, not a replacement for human expertise. Its true power lies in how you combine its capabilities with your creativity, knowledge, and vision.

This FAQ serves as a practical companion to the book, helping you overcome challenges and maximize the value of ChatGPT. If you have additional questions or unique use cases, revisit the relevant chapters for deeper insights or reach out to AI communities to continue your learning journey.

www.ingramcontent.com/pod-product-compliance
Lightning Source LLC
Chambersburg PA
CBHW061323031225
36156CB00022B/1183